The Universal Bead

Joan Mowat Erikson

The Universal Bead

Drawings by Mary Austin

W · W · NORTON & COMPANY

NEW YORK · LONDON

Color photographs by David Rosenthal

Library of Congress Cataloging-in-Publication Data
Erikson, Joan M. (Joan Mowat)
The universal bead / Joan Mowat Erikson ; drawings by Mary
Austin.
p.   cm.
Includes index.
ISBN 0-393-31005-1
1. Beads—Miscellanea.   2. Beads—Folklore.   I. Title.
GT2250.E7   1993
391'.7—dc20   93-16944   CIP

W. W. Norton & Company, Inc.
500 Fifth Avenue, New York, N.Y. 10110
W. W. Norton & Company Ltd
10 Coptic Street, London WC1A 1PU

Printed in the United States of America

1   2   3   4   5   6   7   8   9   0

For Erik

Contents

Plates

Necklace—brass bells, glass beads (Ivory Coast). *Courtesy of The Ethnographic Museum, Basel, Switzerland*

PAGES 87–94

"Smiling" Figure (Veracruz, Mexico). *Courtesy of The Museum of Primitive Art, New York*

"Powhatan's Mantle"—deerskin cloak embroidered with marginella shells. *Courtesy of The Smithsonian Office of Anthropology*

Woman's Dress—deerskin, porcupine quills, beads (Saskatchewan, Canada; Cree). *Courtesy of The Peabody Museum, Harvard University*

Marginella shell embroidered fabric (Florida). *Courtesy of The Smithsonian Office of Anthropology*

Maya Figures (Campeche, Mexico). *Courtesy of The Museum of Primitive Art, New York*

Bag—buffalo hide (North American Indian). *Courtesy of The Smithsonian Office of Anthropology*

Chippewa Delegates from White Earth Reservation, Minnesota, to Washington, D.C., 1911. *Courtesy of The Smithsonian Office of Anthropology*

Necklace—turquoise, coral, ancient dark brown and white beads of unknown origin (Tibetan woman, New Delhi)

PAGES 125–132

Necklace—bone, beads, sennit (Fiji Islands). *Courtesy of The Museum of Primitive Art, New York*

Necklace—ivory, black-and-white glass beads (Alaska; Eskimo). *Courtesy of The Museum of Primitive Art, New York*

Necklace—glass beads, leopard teeth (Republic of the Congo). *Courtesy of The Ethnographic Museum, Basel, Switzerland*

Necklace—disks of black kokos and white conus shell with a pendant of tridacua shell (Gilbert Islands). *Courtesy of The Ethnographic Museum, Basel, Switzerland*

Shell Ornament (California Indians). *Collection of the University of California, Berkeley*

Arm Band—beads of glass, banana seeds, and shell; palm leaf strips; ornament of conus shell (New Guinea; Massim). *Courtesy of The Ethnographic Museum, Basel, Switzerland*

Necklace—sea urchins (Western Islands; Wuwulu). *Courtesy of The Ethnographic Museum, Basel, Switzerland*

Necklace—pearl shell (Philippines). *Courtesy of The Ethnographic Museum, Basel, Switzerland*

PAGES 156–163

Drinking Hara—horn, beads (Cameroun). *Courtesy of The Museum of Primitive Art, New York*

Bead Work (Egypt; Twenty-fifth Dynasty). *Courtesy of The Ashmolean Museum, Oxford*

Doll—wood, seeds, glass beads, cowrie shells, fiber (Cameroun). *Courtesy of The Museum of Primitive Art, New York*

Shrunken Head—feather and beetle-back ornamentation (Jivaro, Ecuador). *Courtesy of The Peabody Museum, Harvard University*

Boy's Initiation Mask—wood, cowrie shells, red kisi seeds (Mali; Bambara). *Courtesy of The Museum of Primitive Art, New York*

Ornament—shells, fiber, paint, cane (Papua, New Guinea). *Courtesy of The Museum of Primitive Art, New York*

Ibeji Figure—wood, cloth, cowrie shells, beads (Nigeria; Yoruba). *Courtesy of The Museum of Primitive Art, New York*

Evil-Eye Charm—shell money, glass beads (New Ireland). *Courtesy of The Ethnographic Museum, Basel, Switzerland*

BETWEEN PAGES 176–185

Choker and Earrings—gold and Pre-Columbian jade (Mexico).

Necklace—turquoise (Arizona) and coconut shell disks (Africa).

Donkey Beads—blue glass trade beads strung with wooden dividers (Far East).

Necklace—amber (Russia).

Beads—Pre-Columbian jade (Mexico).

Necklace—ancient Peruvian beads.

Necklace—carnelian and silver (Indonesia).

Wooden Prayer Beads (Far East).

Blue Glass Beads and Bells (Africa).

Camel's Nose Ring (Middle East).

Mule-driver's Earring (Tibet).

All beads in the color plates are from the collection of Joan Erikson. Photographs by David Rosenthal.

Preface

I WORK WITH gold and silver, precious and semiprecious stones. I
design and make jewelry. At my workbench planning, dreaming up
a pair of earrings or a necklace, I have become aware of the special
attraction of what are probably the simplest forms with which I
work—beads. The problem of incorporating them into a design is
one of treating them with due respect—of letting them, as it were,
speak for themselves in appropriate but uncluttered surroundings.
It is challenging to string them in such a way that by rhythmic
repetition and alternation, by careful or playful arrangements, each
bead preserves its own uniqueness while increasing the charm of the
whole necklace. Old, worn, uneven, and obviously handmade beads

have a special individuality while maintaining a simple directness of form.

The cluster of beads in front of me—turquoise from Persia, dark-veined and brilliant in color; warm coral from the Mediterranean; jade from Mexico, gray-green and ancient; honey-colored amber; iridescent, luminous pearls from India or Japan—have made their way to my workbench from distant places. Some of them are very old, all have been formed with painstaking care and considerable skill, all have been worn before; they have obviously been treasured and have survived. I now share them with their previous owners and in this there is a sense of companionship with the past and a wish, now that it is my turn, to enhance their present form and insure their future. But why should working with beads be so fascinating? What is there about the simple bead that charms both craftsman and wearer?

With curiosity as my first guide I began to visit museums and libraries to ask questions and listen to the experience of others. And I was astonished at the sparseness of catalogued information on this subject. A wealth of material is hinted at in the accounts of ancient and modern travelers, in the reports of archeologists, anthropologists, and historians. But no book devoted to beads alone or to the special role they have played in human affairs was to be found.

So I became a bead bookworm, glancing quickly at the title of a book and then moving directly to its index to see if the little word "bead" was listed there. I have struggled through a long inventory of items found in an ancient Chinese burial only to be rewarded with the tantalizing statement that "there were also beads"; I have read an explorer's account of a great conquest accomplished in its early stages by a handful of beads, yet without a single word describing the beads themselves. Throughout the scattered literature we are given a sense of the power of beads, but rarely are we given any hint of why they should be buried with a person of high rank, how they could move people to an extraordinary output of hard labor, or why they could be exchanged for vast stretches of land.

Such frustration in research is discouraging, but is offset by occasional rewarding encounters. For example, there was the gracious Tibetan woman in the public market of Delhi who wore a handsome necklace of turquoise and coral and told me that her really valuable beads were the two dark-brown and white ones which had belonged to her grandmother. They had been found in the ground, so she said, and were a natural wonder because they had been magically pre-formed and pierced. Their protective powers

Tibetan bead of mysterious origin

would guard her; they were her greatest treasure. Since this is almost precisely the story that natives in West Africa tell about the source of their prized "aggri" beads, and since it is reasonably certain that the aggri bead was imported there in very ancient times from Egypt or Mesopotamia, one may surmise that these Tibetan beads are also very old indeed, the survival of some long-forgotten burial. What a tantalizing challenge to trace those beads! But Tibet . . .

This preoccupation reactivated my interest in the sociological study of art and in problems of human motivation, leading me to consider the possible significance of the role beads have played in human history. But research on beads only turns a host of little questions into some large and complicated ones. Museum curators when asked about the ancient jewels in their collections often confess a very limited store of information; archeologists are seldom able to date a specific bead. Yet the very difficulty encountered in trying to locate these tiny objects in their own time and place only testifies to their long and intricate travels. If relatively little is known of them, it is exactly because they have always been taken so much for granted. In historical writings beads have been treated as objects of slight importance, even when they could be used to buy men and countries, were manufactured by the ton, and filled the holds of ships. But we shall try to piece this history together: where and how beads have been made and of what materials; how and where they have been transported and to what purpose.

Thus the following study cannot be more than an introduction to the story of beads. I am well aware that I have only skimmed a vast surface, pausing here and there, reaching out for information in a somewhat random way as I reacted in pleasure and surprise at the versatility of my subject. Since I am a craftsman more than a scholar, my libraries have included market places and artists' studios, museum exhibits and city streets—which are, after all, the artists' source of material. If the book has an underlying theme, it is that beads somehow link people together and express their common humanity, not only in the sense that they have always been the close companions of people on their travels, but also in the sense that they have had a timeless appeal to all people everywhere. The knowledge that aesthetic satisfactions are common to us as a species, and mark our humanness, will, I hope, shine through the data strung together in this book.

I owe thanks to many people who have offered generous encouragement or have read the manuscript critically. Barbara Joseph graciously contributed much of the material presented on turquoise. So many others have been helpful that I do not know how to express the extent of my gratitude. It is with special appreciation, however, that I thank Paul Perrot of the Corning Museum of Glass and Bernard Bothmer of the Brooklyn Museum, whose letters of introduction to colleagues in other parts of the world made it possible for me to photograph collections of ancient beads in Athens, Rome, Paris, Marseilles, Basel, London, Oxford, and Cambridge. Dr. Alfred Buehler made me welcome at the Ethnographical

Museum in Basel and provided me with many fine slides of the beads in the museum collection. Arthur Woodward made his excellent library on the American-trade beads available to me and permitted me to photograph his collection. I thank them warmly.

The pages you have just read were written when this book was first published. And now, twenty-three years later, how is this ubiquitous bead faring? One thing I would wager is that those dusty boxes in the basements of museums have all been resurrected and reestablished in loftier spaces. For this assumption I lack evidence; a close to ninety year old researcher might well find those depths and cardboard containers too strenuous a challenge.

But statistics are telling—let me offer some I have recently gathered. There are now, I am told, at least twenty bead societies in just this U.S.A. Numbers quoted may well all be approximate since there has been such a steady increase in interest. There are twelve scholarly, twenty general, and many "how-to" books listed about beads, most of them richly illustrated. There are four research-oriented organizations, a quarterly magazine *Ornament*, and a scientific journal *Beads*. In my immediate area of Cambridge and neighboring towns it is estimated that there are nine bead stores offering the public a wide variety of foreign and local beads, many of innovative craftsmanship using new and surprising materials. Bead workshops are also thriving. Encouraging originality and creativity, they offer instruction in the making of beads, and in bead stringing and display.

Add to the above figures recent record participation at bead society conferences. For example, the Bead Society of Greater Washington, D.C., planned for an audience of three hundred people to attend their 1990 bead conference "Beads, Trade, and History," and to their great surprise seven hundred participated.

This surge of interest in beads is astounding. I take personal pleasure in the enthusiasm of newly converted bead fanciers and I am more than pleased if I have contributed to this flourishing of interest. However, it seems important to add a word of caution. Beads have been a source of delight because of the magic of their playfulness and eye-catching fascination for old and young. Truly ancient beads link us to ancestors both known and unknown. Our awareness of their antiquity binds us with their past, which can be awesome. Beads have served many purposes! But mass production and commercialization pose the danger of stealing the charm and power which placed their uniqueness outside the ordinary everyday world of practicalities.

Of course, old, rare, well-formed beads never really lose their original power. I am amazed by the amount of travel to remote parts of the world that has been undertaken in search of unusual beads. Truly venerable ones still evoke ardent research and remain high on the lists of those most desirable and treasured. A glamor clings to objects painstakingly created and those that have been worn like talismans or guarantors of good fortune. I love them for the joy they have given to both those who fashioned them and those who wore and cherished them as personal insignia of delight in beauty and well-being.

So viva the ubiquitous, venerable, enduring, universal bead!

Cambridge, Massachusetts
January 1993

The Universal Bead

I

Caravan, Mule Pack, and Cargo

ON THAT NOT SO DISTANT DAY when we send our first man into space to visit an inhabited planet, with what offering should we provide him to assure his welcome? Even if the beings whom he encounters have mouths and ears as we, he will, most probably, not be able to speak with them. If they do have eyes, however, history suggests our answer—he should offer them a string of colorful glass beads. For the exploration of this world has been accomplished in the past with the aid of shining beads—beads of all the colors of the rainbow. They possess a magic and exert an appeal which touches on some deep longing in the inhabitants of this earth.

If we ask the anthropologist where beads have been used,

his answer is—in every part of the world where man is known to have lived. And for how long have they been worn? The archeologist would answer—since prehistoric times. The earliest graves have yielded remains of ancient necklaces, and the oldest carved statuettes yet unearthed of ancient mother goddesses portray naked female figures wearing necklaces of beads. Since the delight in wearing beads seems to have diminished little over thousands of years we may well ask to what they owe their universality.

JEWELRY, because it is worn on the person, has fallen heir to more than its full share of ridicule and moralizing. Of all the manifestations of creative art, it has lent itself most obviously to the expression of exhibitionism and vanity, of what Veblen called "conspicuous consumption." The names that have been assigned to it in the languages of the Western world—"joyas," "bijou," "trinket," "bauble"—suggest that men have tried to hold it lightly, almost apologetically, as though their pleasure in it might suggest childishness. Yet the fact remains that it has played a surprisingly important role in history. The early trade routes from the Mediterranean to the Baltic Sea were called the "Amber Routes," and included in the barter for Manhattan, as we have all been taught, were strings of glass beads. Why did the sailors of the ancient world risk their lives for amber, and why did Indian hunters so urgently wish to acquire colored beads?

The answer is an illusive one. Graves do not tell us why certain things were buried with their owners; but we may conjecture, as we must, that the articles buried with men or women were their most personal and cherished possessions. Beads were small durable objects placed on a less durable body to accompany the immortal soul to some unknown future estate. To interpret their message could mean to know something more of those who wore them—something of the way in which they faced life as well as death. Let us remember, too, that the wearing of beads has only recently and in our Western world become a prerogative of women. Men in other societies and in other periods of history have worn quantities of beads—and this, in fact, to emphasize masculinity and virility. The young people of today who have audaciously reintroduced the wearing of beads as an expression of anti-establishment solidarity and as a symbol of peacefulness may change these accepted patterns—who can say? But before one can hazard even a guess as to why beads have been so universally desired it will be necessary to know something of the history of their travels with men, of the role that they have played in human affairs. In this chapter, then, I will take the reader from place to place over long distances, and back and forth through the centuries. Such an account will unavoidably be at times both bewildering and repetitious since only thus will it accurately reflect the ubiquity of beads. They have "spoken to" widely separated people expressing identical values and have become "coin" of a universal realm.

Ancient beads of amber and carnelian

The strange and musical names of the faraway places of the world—Zanzibar, Sumatra, Sarawak, Madagascar, Mombasa, Malabar—have enchanted Western ears for centuries. These were places described in the accounts of such early travelers as Marco Polo, Lodovico di Varthema, Duarte Barbosa, and Periplus, and also woven into the fanciful web of the adventures of Sinbad the great sailor. And what were the images evoked by the magic of these place names? Were they bright with peacock colors and glamorous with rich perfumes and tinkling bells? Certain it is that they were associated with the exotic luxuries of the East which the people of Europe have consistently desired. Marco Polo was a merchant, and the account of his trip with his uncles abounds in notes on merchandise—rubies in Balashan, turquoise in Kierman, earrings of gold in Bascia and silver mines in Ydifu, pink pearls in Japan and in Ceylon, rubies, sapphires, topazes, garnets, and amethysts. The story of the travelers' return after years of adventure presents them as dressed on their arrival in Venice like ragged beggars with packs on their backs. But after persuading their reluctant relatives to take them in—so the story goes—they assured their welcome by opening the seams of their rough garments and releasing a hidden treasure of gems and pearls.

The moral of this story, whether it is the fabric of fancy or not (and there is good reason to accept it), is that valuable objects are easiest and safest to transport if they are small and durable.

Silks, spices, gems, ivory, and indestructible, spellbinding, useless gold—these were the contents of the packs in the camel caravans plodding the routes connecting Asia, India, and Africa, and also in the holds of the seagoing ships which finally circled the globe. These were the luxuries which somehow made all the difference in men's lives. But what did the civilization of the West send out to offer as trade goods, since the coins used as currency in those days were of little value outside the lands of their origin? We know that Columbus took with him as trade "truck" a large supply of glass beads and that they served him well.

We also know that Columbus had a Latin version of Marco Polo's journeys, and that, therefore, some of his cargo may have been suggested to him by the notes of this early and observant traveler. He was headed for India and the spice islands, and since Vasco da Gama sailed for the same parts via South Africa and Magellan via the tip of South America, it is not unlikely that their cargoes were similar.

Possibly some of the men who undertook these voyages were motivated more by curiosity and the call of adventure than by mercenary gain. The men who built and equipped the ships and backed the expeditions, however, were enterprising businessmen who were willing to take the financial risks because of the vast profits expected. Vast profits result when you succeed in trading the trifles of your own economy for the rare luxuries of other lands which then bring the highest prices at home. And so our attention is drawn back to those small, durable, universally acceptable and enchanting glass beads which could be manufactured in quantity for a song.

The accounts of men like Marco Polo in the thirteenth century and Duarte Barbosa, a Portuguese who wrote a description of the coast of East Africa and Malabar in the sixteenth century, fired the imagination of the European merchants and gave impulse to trade and exploration. Trade, however, on an earlier, smaller scale, had been flourishing for centuries between East and West. The traders apparently were not very literary and probably did not keep exact accounts, for we have few records of early travel and transactions before the thirteenth century A.D.

Archeologists, then, are the historians of the ancient past to whom we must look for the clues which can help us trace the routes connecting widely separated peoples. They literally dig into unrecorded periods of early civilizations and draw their knowledge from the objects which they bring to light. The land of Sumer, for example, in southern Mesopotamia in the delta of the Euphrates River, has yielded to archeologists the oldest record we have of an agricultural people. The earliest sites which have been excavated

—and we are speaking of prehistoric times here, perhaps as early as 5000 B.C.—produced evidence that these people used stone tools, reared flocks of sheep, and, according to Leonard Woolley, in *Digging Up the Past*, "men and women alike loved to wear strings of beads, simple disks chipped out of soapstone, shell or yellow carnelian."

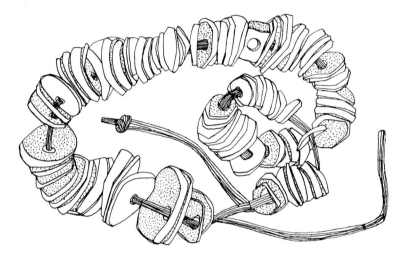

Crudely formed ancient disk beads

The development of an ancient civilization which could produce works of art so rich and technically perfect as those of Ur presupposes a number of factors. There must be a plentiful food supply, well-organized protection against attack, some rather highly developed skills, and sufficient communication with the other lands to make possible continued enrichment and exchange of ideas, techniques, and new materials. Nothing is known of the trade routes which connected Ur with her neighbors, but the later graves of the great dynastic periods which have been excavated yielded objects of gold, silver, lapis lazuli, and carnelian. Since carnelian occurs in the earliest tombs we may suppose that it was available at not too great a distance. Lapis lazuli, however, is not found in or near Mesopotamia. It was imported from the Pamir mountains through Persia to be worked by the Ur craftsmen, and Leonard Woolley tells us that "the great quantities of it found in the royal cemetery prove the importance at that early date of an overland commerce carried on over so vast an area and across so many countries."

Mesopotamia and Egypt were bound together with trade routes so early that it has been impossible to confirm the origin of such inventions as faience and glass. The faience bead dug up in Egypt, which has been dated at 4000 B.C., seems to have a contemporary counterpart in, for example, Assur with the same probable date. The earliest glass beads, dated at 2500 B.C., which are rare and found only one to a grave in Mesopotamia, occur with a similar date and with the same rarity in Egypt, and predynastic beads of lapis lazuli appear there also, although Egypt produced none. The faience beads of Egypt traveled to the far ends of the world, and when glass beads were produced in quantity they too became great travelers.

That Phoenician ships carried trade articles to and from Egypt as early as the Third Dynasty (2500 B.C.) is attested to by the fact that objects from Egypt have been identified among the remains of the Mycenaean epoch in Greece and products of the workshops of Crete have been found in Egypt. Slaves and gold were imported from Africa, and there is some indication of early trade with India. The spread of beads, in fact, is both the hope and the despair of the student of trade routes, for it is very difficult indeed to date these little objects when it is not known how long they were in circulation before they were buried with their owners or where they came from originally.

The graves of Egypt do, however, afford the most comprehensive record thus far available of the development of the craft of bead making, and this knowledge may in time make it possible to trace the ancient trade routes, as well as the origin and the date of manufacture of various types of beads, more accurately.

A bead detector with which we could bring to the surface the lost treasure of the world would produce a fascinating pattern on the face of the globe, the network of ancient commerce—a pattern strung together by beads. The European trade routes would be dotted with amber, the mountain passes of Asia with carnelian and turquoise. From lost Spanish galleons the jade and gold of the Aztecs and Incas would be recovered, and the rivers and portages of the northern fur-trade routes would produce glass trade beads from overturned canoes. Men have, like Hansel and Gretel (but in this case by accident), marked their trade trails by the loss and burial of beads. But lacking such a practical device, the sometimes bewildering routes must be traced by gathering together the rather sparse evidence available.

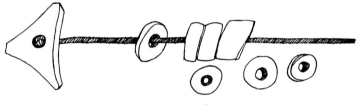

Ancient amber forms

The amber routes, however, have been carefully studied and will provide a mapped beginning.

THE AMBER ROUTES

On the continent of Europe early trade routes can be traced, and here the problem is somewhat less complicated because one article remains so constant that the routes derive their name from it—amber. Close to areas around the Baltic Sea where it is found, Old Stone Age burials yield many amber ornaments, mainly beads and amulets; and amber beads have also been found in graves in Moravia, France, and Austria dating from the same period. During the New Stone Age (3000–1900 B.C.), however, there are indications that Baltic amber traveled as far as Russia, England, and Spain. From Spain it may well have reached Mycenae and Crete.

It is unlikely that we will ever know more about how amber first reached the Mediterranean but we do know that once men had seen it the demand for it was tremendous. Quantities of beads and small carved figures have been found in early graves in Greece and on the Greek islands one tomb at Kakovatos dating from 1600 B.C. yielded as many as five hundred amber beads.

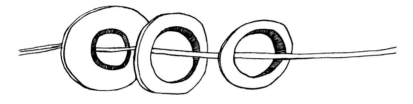

Large amber beads

By 1800 B.C. the Mediterranean peoples were well advanced in the Bronze Age, and their artisans had mastered the art of metal-working and had learned how to produce the alloy called bronze. The raw materials for its production—copper and tin—were available to them from central Europe; what they wanted from northern Europe was amber. The men of the north, in turn, were understandably eager to get this strong, durable metal for tools and arms.

Thus it comes about that the archeological record of the distribution of specific types of bronze and amber makes it possible to trace this route accurately from Jutland into Italy following the courses of rivers and over mountain passes. There were three such routes, the central one leading from Jutland on the west coast of Denmark along the Elbe River to Bohemia across the Brenner Pass into Italy, where ports existed to transfer the amber by sea to the whole Mediterranean area. This route was known and used from about 1750 B.C. on. One marvels at the dedicated tenacity of men, both those who created such a route and carried on the hazardous trade, and those scholars of today who thousands of years later prove by meticulous investigation that the trade did indeed follow this specific course.

There was also a so-called western amber route which came into existence somewhat later. It, too, began in Jutland but branched off westward following the Rhine to Basel and to the headwater of the Danube. The most northerly point of the eastern amber route was near the mouth of the Vistula in Poland and the course of this route led to the upper Adriatic Sea near present-day Trieste.

It is difficult for us even to try to imagine what travel in the continent of Europe may have been like in the times when these routes were developed. The forests were primeval, the rivers without bridges. What we call a route may at best have resembled a foot path or donkey path such as those that still connect the small hill towns in southern Europe. No doubt pack animals were used, and perhaps there were semiprotected campsites where armed guards could watch over both man and beast at night.

In the days of Roman power we think of roads where soldiers could walk abreast with occasional forts as stopping places. But the routes we are discussing existed hundreds of years prior to the up-surge of Rome and may only have been passable in summer. How astonishing then is the quantity of amber which has been found in the Mediterranean area, since it can only be a negligible part of the total amount brought there by such arduous means.

Amber—soft-glowing, mysterious, golden—what kind of a spell did it cast over men? What did it do for people that nothing else nearer at hand could do? We are not likely to find an easy and obvious answer, for though in the literature amber is often men-tioned and described, its desirability is just taken for granted. Perhaps the implication is that the craving for such things is simply and na-turally human and of course universal. But why?

The facts we do know: These routes having been opened hun-dreds of years before recorded history for the purpose of bringing amber from the Baltic Sea to the Mediterranean, and thus connect-

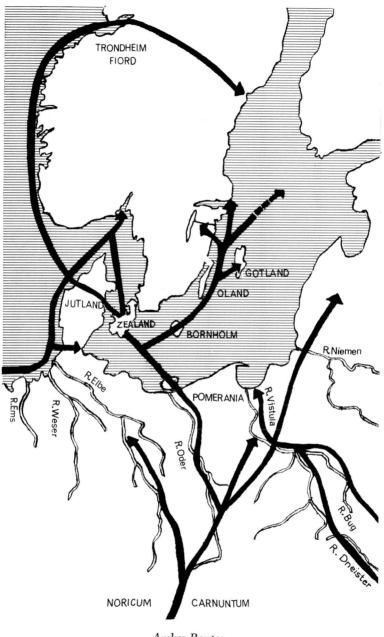

Amber Routes

(FROM SIR MORTIMER WHEELER, ROME BEYOND THE IMPERIAL FRONTIERS)

ing the vast lands beyond the Alps with the culturally more advanced countries of the south, became a major civilizing force in northern Europe. We are told by historians that this trade was the "life blood" whereby the great civilizations of Minoan Crete and Mycenaen Greece was "pulsed throughout the veins of our continent to the young peoples growing up in the north."

Amber disks

ANCIENT TRADE ROUTES TO THE FAR EAST

Earlier in this chapter I mentioned the fact that some knowledge was available to Columbus and the great navigators of that day of the nature of the riches available in the spice islands and India and that they also were informed as to what trade goods might profitably be exchanged with the natives of these lands. Trade had been carried on in spite of hardship and danger between the Orient and the Western world since ancient times and a fund of detailed facts had, no doubt, filtered down perhaps only verbally from captains and sailors to their people at home port.

As we have already seen, the Sumerians were in touch with distant sources of precious stones, gold, and silver, and Egypt, too, had reached south for gold and west for gems and spices before the area of the Mediterranean Sea produced the civilizations of Mycenae, Greece, and Rome. We have evidence that before our era the Dravidians had sailed the Indian Ocean, visiting the Gulf of Aden and the east coast of Africa. The Indian wares were brought to the Arabian port of Sokotra near Guardafui and from there were taken overland to Egypt by the Arabs, who monopolized the lucrative trade in muslins, precious stones, and spices. Zanzibar, off the east coast of Africa, provided a harbor in ancient times for the weary and thirsty sailors of these hot seas, for she was rich in shade and water. This green and fertile island has been a major trading place for two thousand years or longer, and excavation and study in the ports of Arikamedu and Kuala Salinsing in India in recent years have produced evidence of their important historic role in ancient African-Indian trade. There is evidence too that India traded with her neighbors to the north, since Egyptian and Syrian beads brought from the West found their way, probably through India, to China and Japan. Not long ago a Hittite bead was identified in a collection in Jahora; and in Borneo antique beads (the most valued possession of their native wearer) were reliably appraised as glass of early Venetian manufacture—centuries old and still treasured.

The sea route to India from Africa was a tedious and hazardous one, involving months of travel at the mercy of unpredictable winds which alternately battered the ships or left them on the high seas hopelessly becalmed. In the middle of the first century A.D. a sailor by the name of Hippalus made the discovery that these winds were not simply the servants of fickle fate but that they followed a definite seasonal pattern. The great monsoon winds of Periplus could blow ships directly and strongly to the south during the European winter and northeast again from June to September. This knowledge made the still long and dangerous trip more predictable.

To understand why such arduous journeys were undertaken, however, we must know something about the cargo of these ships. From Africa the rest of the trading world has consistently wanted gold, ivory, and slaves. Ivory the Indians did have, and it was used lavishly as a material for ornament and adornment and for carved semiutilitarian objects, but it was perhaps not available in the quantities needed and therefore the rich resources of Africa may have been welcome. There is no question about the need and desire of the Indian princes for gold, the substance prized above all others for decorating objects and making jewelry. The immense riches of the princes of India in gold and gems have been proverbial, although the source of the gold has never been clearly known since only a fraction was mined in India itself.

In this connection it is interesting to note that the ancient Bono gold weights from the African gold coast had two origins, India and Portugal. The use of the Portuguese basic weight is readily understandable since the Portuguese dominated the trade in West Africa for hundreds of years from 1482 onward. But it is less easy to understand where these people learned the Indian system of weights unless one assumes that they are a remnant of prehistoric contact with traders from ancient India.

If Africa was a source of some of India's gold, an idea which is both fantastic and plausible, what did the Africans receive in barter for this gold and for ivory? Textiles, surely, in some quantity. But it is unlikely that Indian spices would have found a ready market in southern Africa since the demand for spices arose largely from the massing together of people in cities and towns with resulting transportation problems and spoilage of perishable foods. However, beads abound in Africa—quantities of carnelian and agate beads are found in the northeast and west, and there is evidence to support the belief that almost all of these were shipped in from Cambay in Gujerat, a city once a seaport, situated north of Bombay. This bead-manufacturing center has been in existence some five thousand years and still continues to produce carnelian beads in large quantities. The raw material comes from Ramtanpur and the lapidaries in Cambay learned early how to treat the paler agate in order to deepen the red color, to shape the beads attractively, and to bring them to a high polish.

Glass beads also abound throughout India. Some of these are very old, and indicate by their type of manufacture, their shape, and their color that they were made there. Recent study in Bombay

State in the newly excavated old town of Brahmapuri shows that glass must have been made there in very ancient times and that beads similar to those found in quantity in Africa were produced there.

This probably explains the fascinating fact that quantities of old beads found around Arab towns like Kilwa Kisiwani and Zanzibar can be dated earlier than the Portuguese traders who later dominated so much of the trade with both East and West Africa. When the Portuguese did come bringing beads from Europe to barter for gold, ivory, and slaves, the Africans at first refused to trade with them and forced them to import beads from India to satisfy their demands. It would be interesting to know if this was a matter of style, a traditionbound taste which values the old and inherited object more than the new. A notation by a later trader seems in any case to verify the importance of ancient style patterns. Jan van Riebeck, who founded the Dutch colony at the Cape of Good Hope in 1651, was unable to use Venetian beads as barter with the Hottentots because they were not interested in acquiring them. He was obliged to have brass beads shipped in from Java.

String of discoidal beads

BEADS AND THE DISCOVERY
OF THE AMERICAS

Historians have always wondered how much information about the Far East had come to the ears of Columbus from other seafaring men. Had he read what Pliny had written about the lucrative trade that could be carried on with India by palming off glass beads as jewels? It is considered possible that he may have been a member of the Portuguese expedition which built Elmira

Castle off the coast of western Africa in 1482, that he had witnessed
trading with the natives of the mainland there, and that his wares
were selected with this experience in mind. Perhaps we shall one
day know the answer to this question, but it is certain that Columbus
felt very sure of his cargo of trading "truck" (as his son rather depre-
catingly refers to it). Christopher Columbus' son, Ferdinand, accompanied him on his first great voyage of discovery, and his account of
this trip includes some of the letters his father wrote to the Spanish
monarchs. In one of the early statements Columbus describes the great
gains to be expected from the new route to India, which he confidently
proposed to chart. "This land is most rich in gold, pearls and precious
stones, and the temples and royal palaces are covered with solid gold."
Later he adds, "When that voyage shall be made, it will be a voyage to
powerful kingdoms and noble cities and rich provinces, abounding in
all sorts of things that we greatly need, including all manner of spices
and jewels in great abundance." He adds, too, that it will be most
opportune to introduce Christianity to the heathen of these rich lands
and one sees a mitre between the two crowns he is addressing.

The *Santa María*, the *Pinta*, and the *Niña* set off then with
their unruly crews of adventurers, their holds filled with "green and
yellow beads, hawk bells, red caps and scissors and mirrors." Every
American child has heard the story of this trip—how wearily long it
was, with what exhaustion and despair the crews faced each landless
day, and how seventy days after first leaving port, land appeared:
solid earth with trees, grass, and fresh water. There were people on
these islands, though, and they came to the shores to see the strange
great vessels. With a show of dignity befitting the emissary of the
Spanish sovereigns, Columbus came ashore. The native cacique
stepped forward to meet the visitor and, no words being possible,
Columbus offered him a string of green glass beads. The gift was
accepted; the Spaniards were made welcome.

These were the people of the Caribbean as Columbus described them in a letter to Ferdinand and Isabella: "They are such

an affectionate and generous people, and so tractable, that I assure Your Highnesses there are no better people or land in all the world. They love their neighbors as themselves, and their speech is the sweetest and gentlest in the world, and they always speak with a smile. They go about naked, men and women, just as their mothers bore them; but believe me, Your Highnesses, they have very good customs, and the king keeps so wonderful a state and displays such dignity that it is a pleasure to watch him. And what excellent memories they have, and how curious they are about everything, asking what such and such a thing is and what is its use."

The Spaniards were eager to trade and the "Indians" bartered what they had and from nearby islands others came to exchange the gold mirrors which they wore about their necks, and pearls and beads.

"After they had conversed for a while, the cacique gave the Admiral eight hundred small figured white, green, and red stone beads together with one hundred figured gold beads, a royal gold crown, and three little gourds filled with gold grains that must have weighed 4 gold marks. The Admiral in turn gave him trading truck that may have been worth 4 reales but had for them the value of 1,000."

And this traffic, so advantageous for the Spaniards, continued. As time went on they became more and more demanding of their hosts, paying less and taking more, until these "affectionate and generous people," exploited beyond endurance, tried to enlist the help of other friendly neighbors to rid themselves of their unwelcome guests.

The Spaniards did move on, finally exploring the coast of Central America and bartering where they could with their green and yellow glass beads and the little tinkling metal bells, which pleased the natives most. The "booty" collected in this way represented a successful trading which gave promise of such sources of further riches inland that other trips were assured. And thus began

Aztec clay beads

the conquest of New Spain.

Cortez asked for and was given permission to follow up the initial explorations made by Columbus. His mandate was to carry out further explorations, to barter with the natives and get information from them about the interior of the land, and of course to convert them to Christianity. Barter they did, and when some of the rich objects from his treasury were sent by Montezuma to satisfy them and speed them on their way home, the sight of these things only whetted their greed and they resolved to risk anything to take the land and all its wealth. How this was done with a force of three hundred men against the Aztec nation by a combination of clever trickery, ruthless perfidy, and lucky coincidence is a tale too long to tell here. But since the bead innocently and gaily played its cheating role in all this, its part in these affairs must be told.

It must be remembered that although the Aztecs were master craftsmen in metalwork and in the carving of stone, they had never seen glass. Their greatest treasure was jade. Green glass must have had a special attraction for them. How friendly it must have seemed to the natives that these strangers should arrive with strings of glass beads as gifts—and as barter. Little did they suspect that these simple transactions were only the prelude to invasion and conquest. With their beads the Spaniards won an initial foothold, and a kind of desperate greed did the rest with the help of horses and gunpowder.

Aztec jade beads

When Montezuma approached the unwelcome visitors who had relentlessly pushed their way to the bridges which surrounded his island capital he accepted them like emissaries of fate and greeted them with dignity. Cortez, who indeed had the courage of a hungry lion, extended to him his gift—a string of glass beads. In return he received gifts of fabulously wrought gold ornaments which by that time the Aztecs knew were what he so urgently coveted.

The history of the conquest and enslavement of a proud people does not give us a rosy view of man the conqueror. The spoils of war, too, in this case, have for the most part been reduced from their original exquisite forms to molten metal and re-formed into coins or other European and more negotiable articles. Almost all of the great loot from the Aztec nation was eventually scattered and lost.

NORTH AMERICAN INDIAN TRADE BEADS

To the north of the Aztec nation stretched a great continent. No advanced civilization had developed on its broad plains or fertile valleys, but tribes of hunters roamed the forests and hills following the game. There were agricultural peoples, too, but their small settlements were far inland to the south and the west. England and France, spurred on by Spain's example, began to eye these lands and lay claim to them.

And these vast new lands were unbelievably rich with game. Hunting was strictly a rich man's sport in England and France. Here in the new world the hunter was rewarded not only by food for himself and his family but also by furs for clothing and for trade. The rich burghers and the nobles of Europe were eager for and paid high prices for furs. So fur-trading companies were formed and given charters by the Crown. Soon the fur traders must have discovered that the natives (also called Indians because Columbus persuaded his contemporaries to entertain, for so long, the idea that this land was part of Asia and that gem-bedecked, golden India would turn up at any moment) were the real hunters. They knew the land and the animal habits and they could adapt themselves to the rugged climate of the northern areas. And the traders took note of what the Indians might want and need in exchange for the skins and furs which they used themselves and parted with only for a price, and what goods they might accept in trade for their lands.

Beads, of course, were acceptable—one might say naturally. The natives of the southern coastlands did not learn about beads nor acquire their fondness for them from their European visitors. They used beads profusely as ornaments, necklaces, arm bands, earrings, and head decorations; and this ornamentation constituted a medium of exchange as well as an evidence of status. They also sewed beads onto strips of deerskin and cleverly wove strands together to form patterned belts and garters. These beads were made of quills, bone, pearls, fish spines, and shells. "They prize highly little beads, which they make of the bones of fishes and other animals and of green and red stones," we are told by the French sailor Le Challeuse. DeSoto was presented with "a necklace of five or six strings of pearls" by a chieftainess who came to meet him on the Savannah River; and another observer records that a Pammikey chief "had a Chaine of pearle about his neck thrice Double, the third parte of them as bygg as pease, which I could not valew less worth then 3 or 400 li had the pearle ben taken from the Muskle as it ought to be." The pearls were obtained from river mussels and from bivalves along the Atlantic coast. The complaint in the quotation above refers to the fact that the Indians opened the shells by heating them over coals, thus damaging the pearls in the process of removing them. The use of pearls extended throughout the Gulf region, but they were sometimes strung for variety with other beads, "rownde pearles, with little beades of copper, or polish bones betweene them."

The bead which served most generally as currency, however, was made of shell. "The Indians had nothing which they reckoned Riches, before the English went among them, except Peak, Roenoke, and such trifles made out of the Cunk shell. These past with them instead of Gold and Silver, and serv'd them both for money, and Ornament," observes historian Robert Beverly. He then goes on to describe these beads. "They are wrought as smooth as Glass, being one third of an inch long, and about a quarter diameter, strung by a hole drill'd thro the Center."* They were of two sorts, light and dark, he reports, the dark ones being the dearer. The infinite patience demanded to make these beads, and especially to pierce them, is also recorded—a manufacturing safeguard which controlled production.

Wampum

That the market was finally flooded by the Dutch and English imitators of wampum, who copied it so successfully with their

* Robert Beverly, *History and Present State of Virginia*

advanced techniques that it could no longer serve as currency, is a later development in the history of the bead in North America.

The white men were not slow to exploit the Indian delight in ornamentation, and specifically their love of beads. These beads were easy to transport, durable, and the most universally acceptable gifts or trade articles on the new continent. When the land-hungry settlers began to arrive along the southeastern coast, they were so few at first that they could not afford to be on unfriendly terms with the native Indians. They bought their toleration and their lands with beads. The early settlers in Virginia at Jamestown were in constant need of supplies of beads for barter with the Indians, who provided them, in exchange, with food, furs, and vast tracts of land. The ships were slow, the need was immediate and great, and so it was decided to set up a glass furnace within the new community. Wood was abundant to keep the hot fires glowing—materials could be found locally or shipped, but artisans were needed. Six Venetian glassworkers were dispatched to Virginia and a furnace was set up, the first glass factory in America. Then the London Company wrote the following cautioning letter:

"The making of beads is one of Captain Morton's chief employments, which being the money you trade with the natives, we would by no means have, through too much abundance, vilified, or the Virginians at all permitted to see or understand the manufacture of them. We pray you therefore seriously to consider what proportion of beads can be vented and their worth not abated."*

Either the glassworkers failed to produce or the beads failed to charm, for on March 22, 1622, the Indians massacred the Jamestown colony and destroyed even the glass furnace. Thus disaster prevented the threatening inflation.

On the northern seaboard, the counterpart of this ill-fated glass-manufacturing enterprise was much more successful. The Dutch and English settlers moved into an area where shell money

* Rogers and Beard, 5000 Years of Glass

was even more generally accepted as currency than in the south, where a greater variety of beads, including those of imported glass, more than sufficed to please the natives.

The form of shell bead designated as wampum—that is, a small cylindrical bead averaging about a quarter of an inch in length by an eighth of an inch in diameter—existed only in very small quantities, north or south, before the arrival of the white man. There were many more discoidal shell beads which, when strung together, closely resemble wampum and may also have been used as currency. These discoidal beads are comparatively easier to form and pierce than the traditional cylindrical wampum, for which the quahog, or hard clam, was used. The quahog shell used for the making of wampum furnished both the white and the highly valued dark-blue or "black" shell core, a substance which was exceedingly hard to cut and all but impossible to drill without sharp metal tools. How this was accomplished before the arrival of the settlers is only surmised, but the Indians were quick to adopt the use of metal to assist them in the drilling process. Even so, their patience and persistence in this task was noted by early writers.

"If this Wampum Peak be black or purple, as some Part of that Shell is, then it is twice the Value. This the Indians grind on Stones and other things till they make it current, but the Drilling is the most difficult to the English man, which the Indians manage with a Nail stuck in a Cane or Reed. Thus they roll it continually on their thighs with their Right-hand, holding the Bit of Shell with their left, so in time they drill a Hole quite through it, which is a very tedious Work."*

By 1641 wampum had become full legal tender in Massachusetts, and Roger Williams in Rhode Island records that six white beads "are current with the English for a Peny" whereas of the "black, inclining to blew, . . . three make an English Peny." In 1648 there were enough ill-made beads on the market to occasion legis-

* Ernest Ingersoll, *Wampum and Its History*

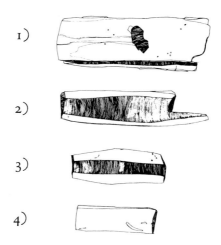

Four steps in the process of making wampum from "cunk shell"

lation in Massachusetts Bay which specified that they "shall be intire without breaches, both the white and the black without deforming spotts." The Indians, we are told, were cautious and astute traders so that this legislation was probably passed to protect the white settlers, who, at the time, used wampum almost exclusively for their transactions among themselves. Judgments of the courts were made payable in shell money, and inventories of deceased colonists commonly included items of wampum.

It followed, then, that the English and the Dutch would recognize a rewarding business opportunity in the manufacture of wampum, and so they did. The Dutch set about to produce wampum—and did so both most expertly and successfully—dispatching it in quantity from New York to the colonists. From along the Atlantic coast the English sent shiploads of shell home, where it was fashioned and returned; and many enterprising individuals, both white and Indian, set up their own wampum industries, which continued in business until the flooded market had abandoned shell beads and was dealing only with glass beads of European manufacture.

Even when wampum was discredited as currency, however, it retained its sacred ceremonial properties. It was a high symbol in all negotiations of Indian tribes with one another and was offered as a record of treaties between Indians and white men, marking the gravity and authority of the transaction. "This belt preserves my words," an Indian chief would declare. Endowed with mystic power and dignity, it was guarded by the chiefs as they would guard the honor of the tribe.

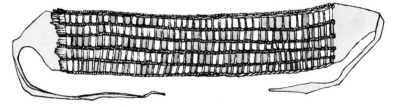

Wampum wristband

Unable as we are to turn to a portrait in color of this early American, ceremonially dressed in his best, we must be grateful for the word picture drawn for us by a contributer to *Newes from New-England*:

"They cut their haire of divers formes, according to their Nation or people, so that you may know a people by their cut; and ever they have a long lock on one side of their heads, and wear feathers of Peacocks, and such like, and red cloath, or ribbands at their locks; beads of wampompeag about their necks, and a girdle of the same wrought with blew and white wampom, after the manner of chequer work, two fingers broad, about their loins: Some of their chiefe men goe so, and pendants of wampom, and such toyes in their ears. And their women, some of the chiefe, have faire bracelets, and chaines of wampom."

The use of wampum as currency gradually gave way in the new colonies to the use of silver coin. A certain amount of it was still produced for Indian trade until late in the nineteenth century, but the great demand had long since petered out. Glass trade beads manufactured in Venice and Bohemia had been introduced and had found a market.

Wampum beads were both sturdy and colorful, incorporating in their way the strength of the sea, its depth of blue and its plumy white. The patterns which the Indians designed with it in their belts and other ornamentation were geometric and clear, a simple but effective contrasting of light and dark. They were heavy beads and hung with sectioned clarity of line against deerskin or weighted the material on which they were sewn. Marked by a quality of austerity even when displayed in quantity, they seemed a fitting designation of rank and power for a proud race.

In contrast, the polychrome glass beads sent from Venice were highly sophisticated, designed with delicate motifs of leaves and flowers. They somehow seem too contrived to be included in the ornamentation of a sacred bundle or to dangle from a tomahawk, and might more fittingly grace an elegant European lady. Strung in a necklace below the painted face of a Crow brave in battle dress, they would probably, to our eyes, have appeared incongruously unferocious. Yet the Sioux, the Blackfeet, the Walla-walla, and especially the Crow Indians apparently used them, paying the high price charged by traders. For these beads were (and still are) made by hand in Murano, which accounts for the uniqueness of each bead.

Polychrome beads

The value of beads differed according to their size, color, and decoration. What individual traders demanded for their beads we will, in all probability, never know, but the Hudson Bay Company has left some meager records which give us an idea of standards of value. All references to value are quoted in terms of "one made beaver," a beaver skin which has been dried and is ready for tanning. A bead of green or yellow glass, about the size of a pea, was valued at six for one made beaver. A somewhat larger light-blue bead had a value of three for a skin; for a large bead of opaque light-blue glass, the trader demanded two skins.

The high prestige of the color blue is clearly recorded, since mention is made repeatedly in accounts of trading with southern and western Indians of the demand for blue beads and blue beads only. The Seminole squaws, when blue glass beads became available, wore as many strings as they were able to afford and could carry around their necks. Young Tiger Tail's wife is described as being bedecked with at least two hundred such strings of blue beads. Of course, she was visiting relatives and was willing, apparently, to forgo moving her head for the satisfaction of being well dressed.

Lewis and Clark, who explored the West, also write of the power of the blue glass bead. Their records note many incidents of Indians refusing to trade at all except for the preferred blue beads. The natives they encountered on their westward trek were already in possession of these glass beads, and there is a challenging note in the journals which suggests that they came from China. One may hazard the guess that they came to this continent in trade during the years of the brisk traffic in sea-otter skins between China and California which nearly resulted in the extinction of the California sea otter. From the Columbia River region Lewis and Clark recorded the following in their Journals: "In the evening Seven indians of the Clot sop Nation came over in a Canoe, they brought with them 2 Sea otter Skins for which they asked blue beads and such high prices that we were unable to purchase them without reducing our Small Stock of Merchandize, on which we depended for Subsistance on our return up this river. Mearly to try the Indian who had one of those Skins, I offered him my Watch, handkerchief a bunch of red beads and a dollar of the American coin, all of which he refused and demanded 'ti-a-co-mo-shack' which is Chief beads and the common blue beads, but few of which we have at this time."

The Crow Indians, we are told, were among the earliest of the Upper Missouri tribes to employ trade beads in their decorative arts, in which they excelled. In the early 1800's they already were in possession of "small blue glass beads that they get from the Spaniards but by the second and third man"—that is, through the Shoshoni, who traded with the Southwest. They too regarded these so highly that they would pay as much as a horse for one hundred blue beads.

Even a bead as complicated in manufacture and as ancient in design as the handsome "chevron bead" made its appearance on this continent. They have been found, though in small numbers, in Canada and Florida and from the east to the west coasts, and even in Mexico, where they were, no doubt, introduced by the Spaniards. Chevron beads appear in collections from ancient Egypt and are highly valued throughout Africa. The bead is barrel-shaped, some as large as a walnut and others only the size of a hazel nut. It is formed of layers of glass—deep blue on the outside, opaque brick red under that, and then a layer of transparent pale green. The layers are themselves separated by thin coatings of opaque white glass. When the bead is ground at the ends, the lower layers are revealed, forming starlike points which are sometimes extended into the sides of the larger specimens. They were designed by an unknown master and have held their own through the fashion changes of centuries.

But the bead which, above all others, took hold of the imagination of the North American Indians was the Venetian and Czechoslovakian seed bead, that small bead which could be sewn onto clothing and which gave Indian women the opportunity for unsurpassed accomplishments in beadwork.

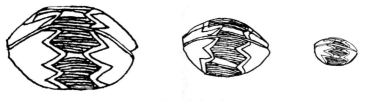

Chevron beads

There was good reason for this preference. The Indians had long been imaginative and skillful in designing with porcupine quills. These they dyed and attached ingeniously to the skins with which their clothing was made. This was most painstaking work but, combined with painting, it resulted in brilliant decoration on the muted background of the deer and buffalo skins. Weaving skills were also known and practiced by Indian women, and the small seed bead could be woven into solid ornaments and sewn onto backgrounds of reinforcing skin or cloth. Beads of bright red, blue, yellow, green, and opaque white were preferred for this work, although a few examples of geometric designs in black and white exist, somewhat resembling the older designs in wampum. The skills developed in this technique were elaborations of the basic one learned by every Boy Scout and Girl Scout today. Taut threads are held, at the desired width apart, between two firm objects; the beads, which are strung on a thread, are passed under this warp and held between the threads while a needle is passed through them again on the surface, securing them permanently in position. Innumerable variations of pattern are possible with this method, limited only by the available colors of beads and the imagination of the weaver. But the technical perfection in the manipulation of threads, and the accuracy and sensitivity to form as well as the combinations of colors displayed in the Indian work, are astonishing and admirable. The quantity of this type of work now in the care of museums may jog us into considering how many, many little bunches of beads—five or six strings, each four to six inches long—valued at "one made beaver" must have traveled to this continent from Europe and been carried by canoe, horse, and pack into the interior.

For the remaining descendants of the early Americans the vast lands and the game are gone, a whole way of life no longer exists. Our Puritan ancestors may have consoled themselves as Columbus had that "the trading truck may have been worth 4 reales but had for them the value of 1,000" but whatever the rationale for the deed may have been, historical conscience cannot escape the fact that a gigantic hoax was perpetrated on initially trusting and friendly peoples. The evidence is offered by the beads themselves that have endured and are now gathered in our museums.

Historical conscience, however, may be put to rest with ease by the simple forgetting of details of what happened long ago. We salute the enterprise and bravery of the conquistadors, and the endurance and uprightness of our Puritan forefathers, and we often tend to bury the shabby deals with the beads. But the history of beads must include a more recent and more flagrant instance of the exploitation of man by man.

BEADS AND THE EARLY
AFRICAN SLAVE TRADE

There is a type of bead found in Africa that has aroused the curiosity of travelers and traders in that country since white men first visited there. This is the so-called "aggri" bead, which has been prized on the west coast and particularly in the Gold Coast area.

The origin of the aggri bead is a mystery. The natives' accounts of its presence suggest something magic and mythical. They maintain that travelers journeying in the far interior at night sometimes see flames rising from the ground, and if they dig in such a spot they will find one or more aggri beads. The belief that they come from the ground is so universal that we must assume it has some foundation in fact. Beads of a similar nature which were excavated at Zimbabwe in Mashonaland were considered by experts to have been Egyptian in origin. It is difficult to describe these beads with any accuracy. They vary in color from semiopaque yellow to various brighter colors, sometimes plain and sometimes designed and variegated. In form they have been described as shapeless masses perforated for stringing, or spherical, ovate and oblong. The material is glass or porcelaneous. But older natives are able to distinguish genuine old aggri beads with unerring accuracy. When a Birmingham firm obtained some samples and tried to reproduce them, they were able to do so to the complete satisfaction of European experts but the natives immediately detected them as frauds. That the traders were eager to obtain a good facsimile in quantity is understandable, for a single bead is said to have been literally worth more than its weight in gold, and they were large and heavy. Among the Ashanti in West Africa the thief who stole one single aggri bead was obliged to pay the owner seven slaves in restitution. Natives were most reluctant to part with them since they were esteemed as heirlooms within the family, a bride perhaps receiving one on her wedding day. Usually they were not worn in strings, as only kings or very wealthy persons were able to display such affluence, but a single aggri might be included in a string of less valuable beads and worn around the neck or wrist.

It is quite inconceivable that these beads were made in western Africa. The refinement of skill in glassmaking required to produce them suggests conclusively that they were imported from a country which had achieved a high degree of virtuosity in glass manufacture. Here again Egypt or Mesopotamia appears as a possible source, and perhaps India, and one wonders when traders first discovered that Africa was rich in gold, ivory, and slaves and that the natives would trade for beads. But it is certain that Africa was renowned as a source of these luxuries before almost anything else about the depths of this great continent was generally known.

It is impossible to date the beginning of the slave trade on the coast of East Africa. All we know is that it began at some time before the beginning of the Christian era, that it was carried on by traders who plied their trade along the coast of the Persian Gulf as far as India and down the coast of Africa, and that black slaves did reach Egypt and the Mediterranean.

The first description which is extant of the eastern coast of Africa was written in the sixteenth century by the previously mentioned Duarte Barbosa, a Portuguese who sailed from port to port making notes of his keen observations. These were Arab settlements, the Arabs having monopolized the trade between Africa and India for hundreds of years. Barbosa describes the towns as rich settlements with fine houses. He also describes the merchant princes of these towns as luxuriously clothed in fine textiles from India and profusely adorned with fine jewels. He speaks of "grey and red and yellow beads, which come to the said kingdoms in other larger ships from the great kingdom of Cambay." In another entry he refers to the "beads of Cambay, which are much used and valued amongst them" and again to "glass beads from Cambay and large and small beads perforated for stringing."*

His extensive journey finally brought him to the coast of India and eventually to Cambay. He states in verification of these

* See *Duarte Barbosa*, edited by M. E. J. Stanley

earlier notations that "there are also great lapidaries, and imitators of precious stones of all kinds and makers of false pearls which seem real." They manufacture "beads of great size, brown, yellow, blue and colored, which they export to all parts." Of Limadura, near Cambay, he writes that here they "make beads for Berberia. It is a stone white as milk, and has some red in it, and with fire they heighten the color, and they extract it in large blocks. In these places there are great artists who manufacture and pierce these beads in various fashions, oval, octagonal, round and of other shapes. [They] carry them throughout all Arabia, Persia and Nubia."

The stone described is undoubtedly carnelian, and the eastern coasts of Africa do indeed abound in carnelian beads in various shades of red and in all shapes and sizes. It is said that up to very recent times carnelian beads could be found in quantity in the ground around the old Arab towns and especially in Zanzibar, which drew the ships of the Indian-Africa routes into her harbor for water and trade.

We have already listed the three valued trade items from Africa—gold, that least useful but universally most highly prized of metals; smooth white ivory, for carving ornamental objects (later used for making quantities of piano keys); and slaves. The slaves from the eastern coast for which the Arab and later the Portuguese traders bartered were usually desired as personal household servants for the wealthy and the princes of Egypt, Asia, the Mediterranean, and India. They were selected for their appearance and health. Women brought higher prices than men and the price was set according to grace, age, and beauty. The knowledge that this traffic went on for hundreds of years makes one recall various previously unexplained images (the beautiful black faces of some of the figures in the Ajunta cave paintings of India and the small black-turbaned pages in the court paintings of southern Europe) and the frequent references to Nubian slaves in the literature of the Mediterranean and the descriptions of black dancing girls in the retinues of the sultans of Persia. In Zanzibar, which was the unrivaled center of this trade, the merchants gathered to select their wares: the traders who traveled into the interior came to deliver their slaves and to select their trade goods, the town thrived, and the king grew rich from the duties he imposed on every transaction.

In the labor market better known in the Western world the trade in slaves developed as the demands grew for laborers to promote plantation economy along the coasts and on the islands of the New World. Any kind of slave whose strength could be exploited in the new sugar or cotton industries was then acceptable. The trade was very profitable for the Arab slave traders, who ravaged the areas inland, setting tribe against tribe and carrying off men, women, and children into captivity. This kind of operation involved little outlay in goods—except perhaps gifts to the chiefs and nobles who entered into the conspiracy in partnership with the slavers. The method was capture by force and threat of instant death to the resisters, the laggards on the march, the weak, the wounded and sick. The caravans were force-marched to the sea from April to November, the dry season, frequently in groups of five hundred but groups of a thousand were not rare.

The currency for any trading which was done inland was cloth, wire, and beads. All the accounts by visitors to the coast or inland areas of East Africa during this period describe the opulence both of the town dwellers and the native chiefs and their households. They developed an appetite for imported textiles, brass wire, bangles, and especially beads, which they wore in great quantities, bedecking their many wives, children, and nobles in colorful array.

Perhaps the most pathetic description is that of the way in which the slaves in Zanzibar were transformed into attractive commodities after their arduous march to the market. They were rubbed with palm oil and then decorated with beads to enhance their appearance and attract buyers. The beads, of course, were removed after the sale.

It is hard for us to believe that this barbarous trade continued at least until 1899, the last slave ship recorded in East African waters having been wrecked in that year off Wasin Island not far from Mombasa.

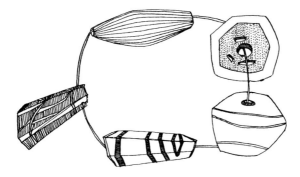

East African beads

No shipping companies have left us records or the bills of lading of trading ships on the east coast of Africa to document the quantity or quality of the beads introduced—perhaps because the dhows used were owned by their Arab captains or by private individuals who accepted verbal accounts of transactions. In any case, no such documentation is as yet available to Western readers. Trade on the west coast, however, early became the domain of companies with charters from the various European countries then competing with one another for the control of the trade of West Africa. These companies had shareholders who demanded increasingly detailed and accurate accountings. The following letters and bills of lading are quoted from *Documents Illustrative of the History of the Slave Trade* by Elizabeth Donnan.

In 1446, Antam Goncalvez, a Portuguese captain, penetrated south to Cape Verde to ransom one Joao Fernandez from a native chief who had intimated that he had Negroes he wished to sell. "And when the noble (Ahude Meymaur) concluded his bargaining, he received some things which pleased him most among those tendered to him by our men (though they were really small and of little value) and he gave us for the same nine Negroes and a little gold dust." This as far as we know was the first recorded instance of the purchase of slaves. What these small articles of little value were we are left to conjecture, but judging by the bills of lading of the ships which later began to trade in earnest one would judge that beads—these smallest but also most consistently mentioned items of little value—were among them. It is interesting to note that even in 1651, when glass beads were available in quantity in Europe, the following instructions were included in a letter from the Guinea Company to James Pope: "Also we have delivered unto Mr. Howard 6 strings of East India Cristall beads, 2 of a round small sort, 2 of a great round sort, and 2 of square cristall, they go for a sample at the request of a good friend, you may sell them to the most advantage and enquire what quantitie will there vend." India was apparently still producing beads desirable for trade in Africa—more desirable perhaps than those which were more easily available in Europe.

By 1678 notation about the kinds of goods most in demand at the trading centers in West Africa became detailed and specific. At Orpha in Arda, on September 17, 1678, for example, we find such items listed—"All Sorts of beads, white, Greene and Lemon Coller the best well strung. . . . Red Corall in Long Beades . . . Bonges (Bowges or cowrie shells)." The items listed as being on hand in the "factory" of Ophra include 4410 menelloes, which are quoted as worth 200 to a slave.

In 1678, "108 bunches of blue Beads" are mentioned as part of a transaction in exchange for "gold, Eleph'ts teeth and slaves." By 1779–81, we find documented the "Invoice of goods laden abord the 'Swallow.' "

"Capt. Evan Seys Commander for accompt of the Royall African Company of England Bound for New Callabar their to take in 220 negroes and consigned unto said Capt. Evan Seys.

```
Iron 2000 barrs
Copper barrs. 5 chests
Cowries 3 barrells
Beeds, 1 chest
            26 bunches white
            17 ditto christall
Manelloes 1 bunch black
5000 rings
For customs and all other charges
1 box  2 scarlett laced coats ⎫
       2 white hatts laced   ⎭  for presents
```

The accounts of the *Mary*, 1680–81, list in even greater detail the beads included in their trade goods:

```
Cowry 50 barrells
Beads 11 chests
          bunches 36 great white
                  66 small white
                  78 Haire collor
                  30 Black
                  61 small black
                  85 great white
                  54 Lemon collor
                  52 reds
                  67 white
                  13 green transparent
                   8 lemon collor
                  87 ditto transparent
                  57 orange
                 100 green transparent
                  25 lemon ditto
                  64 black
                 ─────
                 813      883 bunches
                         220 orange ⎫
                                    ⎬ 320 bunches
                         100 Lemon  ⎭
```

All lists, then, include cowries in great quantity, for without them trade was difficult anywhere along the coast; it was in fact the custom to pay half the agreed price for slaves in cowries and half in European goods. Cowries were currency inland and since the coastal towns were only the centers of sea trade carried on by inland traders some of the goods in each transaction served the purpose of providing the inland traders with commodities desired by the inland chiefs. On the coast the ship traders usually tried to include some of their least valuable cargo in each sale. The price of slaves between the ages of twelve and thirty was established per head with the king or chief of the trading center, for example, men at ten iron bars each, women at nine iron bars, children and older slaves at some agreed lower rate. Trade goods were then selected which were agreed upon as equal to the sum of iron bars. In the early days of the slave-trade ships' captains were sometimes simply informed by the coastal chiefs that there were no slaves for sale. The country had been at peace and there were therefore no captives. The captains then bartered for gold and ivory, and left. Later, when the demand for slaves had become a clamor from the planters of the New World and the price had risen accordingly, and when the coastal chiefs had been supplied with guns and ammunition and had become addicted to rum, there was no more peace in the land. But the price of slaves varied constantly according to supply and demand, the demand being represented by the number of ships in the harbor at any given time. The value of goods fluctuated also according to the cargoes which sometimes flooded the market with one type of merchandise, sometimes another. The necessary cowries were not cheap goods for the trader—they were imported from the Maldive Islands through Liverpool until an enterprising German undertook to ship them from Zanzibar on the east coast of Africa to the west coast. Compared to cowries, beads were fairly cheap for the European traders, who induced their clients to take as many as possible to make up the goods in trade. Judging by the descriptions of the lavish use of beads by the natives of the interior, we must assume that the native traders used them extensively for inland trade. They probably made up the bulk of those easily transportable objects of little value which were so profitable in trade with people who had not been exposed to the more luxurious and costly items in demand on the coast, items such as brandy, guns and powder, and iron bars for making weapons.

That the natives, however, made specific demands as to the color, quality, size, and shape of acceptable beads is also testified to by the records. A trader would set out with certain kinds of beads recommended to him only to find that the natives with whom he wished to do business were entirely uninterested in his particular bead supply. Perhaps he had brought blue beads and found that he should have brought yellow ones, whereupon he would be obliged to get rid of the blue ones in any way possible and at a loss. Returning confidently in another year or so with yellow beads he would discover that blue beads had become fashionable and that no one would trade for yellow beads.

There were, however, some beads which were not subject to fluctuations in fashion, such as the aggri beads and some stone beads which had special magic properties. The cowrie shell maintained its value and prestige as an object of decoration, as a magic symbol, and as currency for hundreds of years.

As the demand for slaves increased in the West Indian sugar plantations the slave trade grew in volume, and toward the end of the seventeenth century and the beginning of the eighteenth, trade commodities included new items to meet the higher prices and more sophisticated demands of the native chiefs. Larger quantities of guns, powder, and spirits are listed in the bills of lading and also swords, belts, and even shoes and slippers are included. But still the cowries are listed in quantity, and the beads appear among goods designated as best suited to the Calabar slave trade. In 1698 the *Dragon* sets off, for example, with five hundred and forty-six pounds of beads, suggesting the great quantity still in demand. There are some noteworthy changes, however; the listings become increasingly selective and specific. Unfortunately, they include some terms which are no longer in general use so that one can have no clear picture of the object desired. The *Armenian Merchant* in 1689 carries "234 Ozs Corra Ps"; the *Hannibal* in 1693 has "rangoes large and red Coral, large smooth and of a deep red"; the *Norman*

Galley in 1714 lists "3 bandes of 159 false corrall." The *King Solomon* out of London, July 1720, carries "Coral and Arangoes 1 trunk —SaPampores and 130 lb. beads." The manifest of the *Dispatch*, Bristol, September 30, 1725, has in her hold "1378 lbs. Bugles [Venetian Beads]" and other lists include "a sort of bugle called Pezant," "Maccatons, that is, beads of two sorts," "Christial pipe beads," and yellow amber.

The beads transported in the slave-trading vessels also served the purpose of ingratiating the captain of the vessel with the king or chief with whom he was dealing. In fact, the gifts for the king with which the captain came ashore were "expected" and the success or failure of his enterprise could well depend on the competition in gifts offered by other slavers and on how acceptable the recipient found these offerings. In John Barbot's *Description of Guinea in 1682*, we find the following account of these transactions:

"The commerce is here adjusted with the king, in the same manner as it is done at Fida; and as soon as a ship arrives there from Europe, the commander or super-cargo must wait on the governor of Little Ardea, to be conducted by him to the king, taking along with him the usual presents, which commonly consist in a parcel of about three or four pound weight of fine coral, six Cyprus cloths, three pieces of morees, and one piece of damask, for the king; another parcel of coral for the queen; a piece of damask napkins for the prince; one piece of armoizin for the Foella or captain of the Whites; another for the porters of the court; another for the courtiers, or else some beads, or great brass rings; ten gal in has of Boejaes for dancers who commonly attend at the waterside of landing; or the value thereof in other things."

When the ship had finished its trading and received its full quota of slaves, the king again was presented with gifts "as an acknowledgment to that prince for his favor." In spite of the baffling language it is clear that beads were consistently important and that the demands of the natives were exacting.

In later years of the eighteenth century the slave trade with the southern states of America and the West Indian islands assumed tremendous proportions, but we no longer have references to exact bills of lading full of weird-sounding items. The trade was for the most part carried on with rum, and there resulted the uncomfortably ironic situation in which slaves were engaged in making produce for the purchase of slaves.

WHEN ONE REVIEWS in his mind's eye the beads of the world—a visual experience in which one can revel in art museums of ethnography—certain distinct configurations of form and color take precedence over more blurry impressions. Clearly defined are the turquoise and coral beads of the Southwest of North America, the glowing amber of the North Sea, the precious stones and pearls of India, the cunningly strung shells of the South Seas, jade from China and Mexico, the blue faience and multicolored glass from Egypt and the Mediterranean. If you then conjure up in your mind or visit a display of African beads the array is dazzling by mere richness of color and contrast. These are not precious or semiprecious stones—they are with few exceptions just beads of humble, cheap glass. But they have been strung with appreciative care and with an attention to arrangement and line that suggests a brilliant vitality and gaiety. There is a riot of color and a careful contrasting of form which is both bold and controlled. It is barbaric, if you will, but it jolts you refreshingly out of visual apathy with much the same impact as that exerted by modern painting. Our color palette of today no doubt is as Africa-inspired as is, indeed, our music.

It is difficult to think of the trade of the past and contrast it in even the most cursory way with the trade of today. Caravans and mule packs, caravels and canoes belong to another world than this of planes, trains, trucks, and tankers. Yesterday's luxuries have turned into everyday necessities so that it is no longer possible to differentiate between them. Perhaps tourism is the greatest luxury

African beads made in Europe

item with which our trade ways cope today and yet, for many areas of the world, tourists are the only cash crop. The faraway places are not very far away from anywhere and previously unheard of names appear in the newspaper daily—but they are now troublesomely close with all the unexotic details of their political and economic problems, which—informative as they are—do not inspire fantasies about tinkling bells and peacocks and beads.

However, anyone who may be harboring the idea that what has been described is a merely historical item now to be seen only in antique shops and museums should observe the fashions of to-today. Obviously beads are being produced in great quantities and are still traveling—only much faster. Men, it is true, in general no longer bedeck themselves with jewelry of any kind but the women of our century—although, or perhaps just because, their costume is severely tailored—wear masses of beads. With colorful gaiety they provide the feminine touch and underscore the uniqueness without which the new equality might prove to be drab, and human relationships to have lost their zest.

Neck Ornament—shell, beads, animal teeth, seed pods, fiber
(Solomon Islands)

Necklace—turquoise, coral (New Mexico; Zuñi)

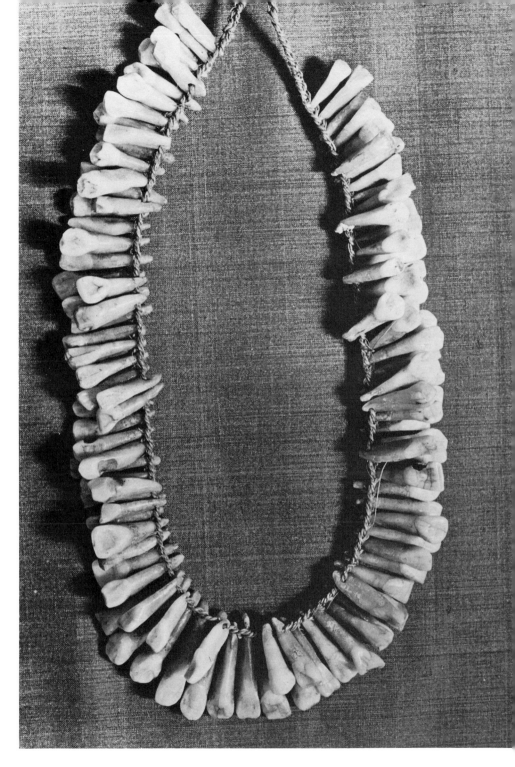

Necklace—human teeth (Gilbert Islands)

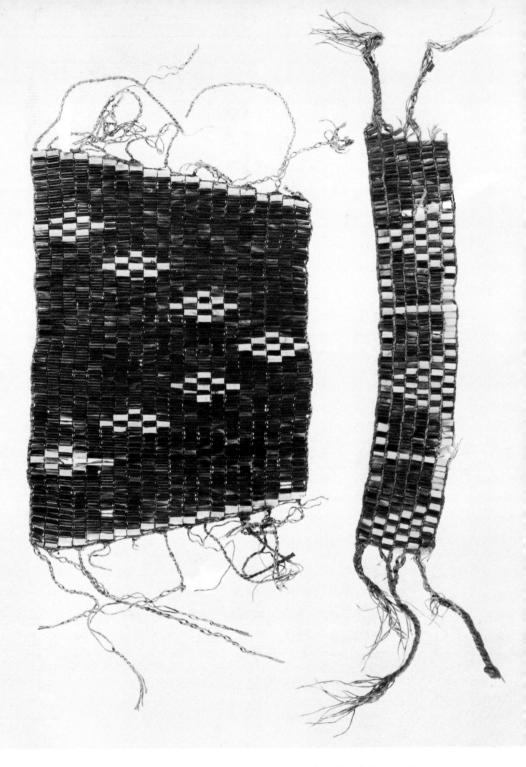

Wampum—wrist ornament or hair band (Iroquois)

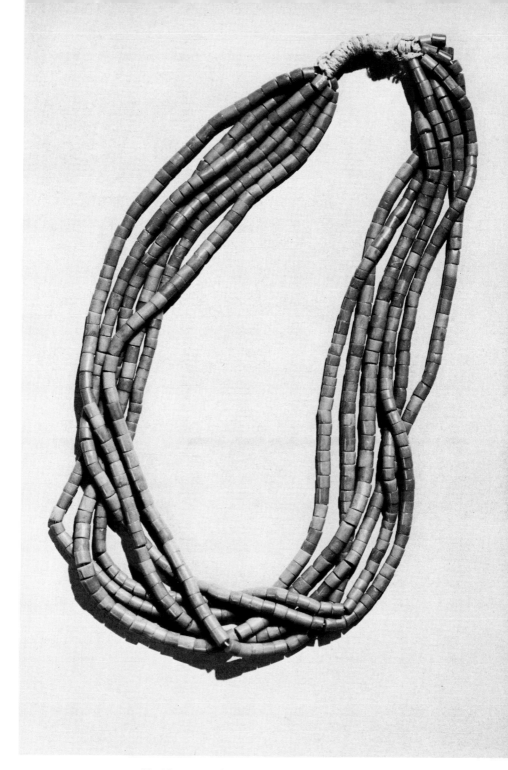

Necklace—coral (New Mexico; Zuñi)

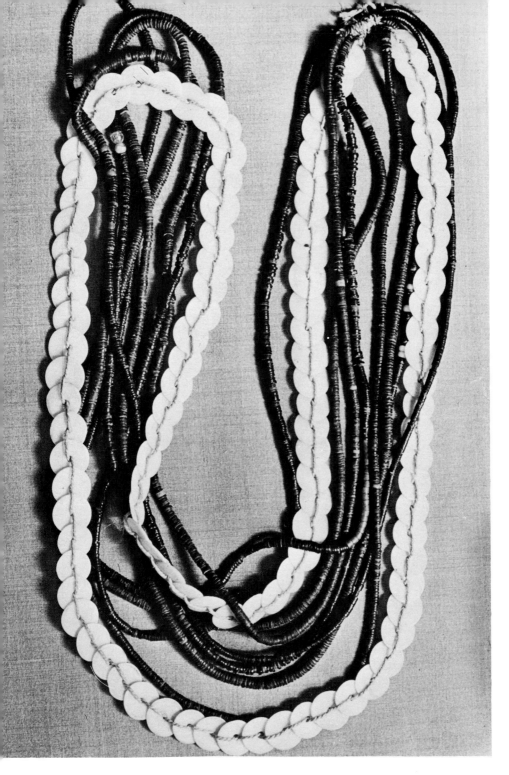

Necklace—palm nut, shells, glass (Brazil; Tupari)

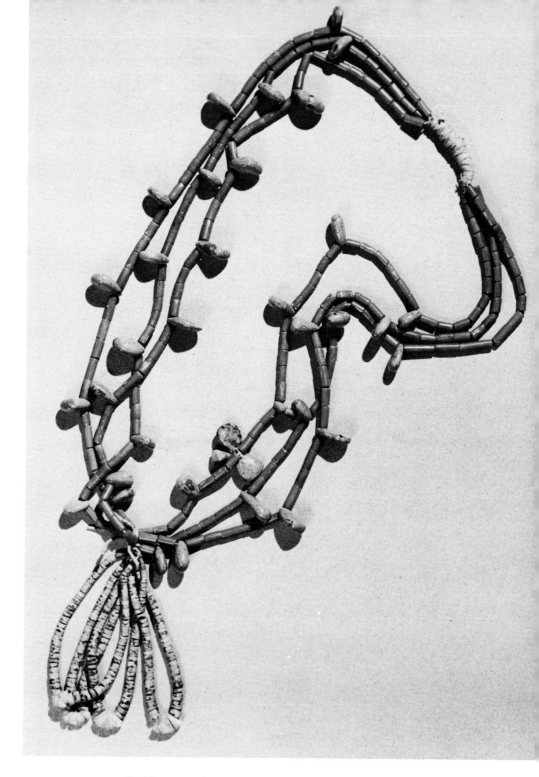

Necklace—coral, turquoise, stone (New Mexico; Zuñi)

Necklace—brass bells, glass beads (Ivory Coast)

The Uses of Beads

THE INHABITED WORLD, then, is and always has been full of beads, and perhaps more than any other single kind of thing they have been meaningful to man as well as attractive, useful as well as ornamental.

They have clothed him or decorated his naked skin; they have served to differentiate his face and body in order to set him apart from his enemies and mark him as one of his own people. Beads have been used as insignia of title, office, rank, and prerogative. They have been endowed with magic, delegated to serve as currency, treasured as wealth. And man has simply enjoyed them.

The early descriptions of the Aztecs as Cortez first saw them

or of the Incas in Peru paint verbal pictures for us of splendidly
bedecked and ornamented personages. Catlin's portraits of North
American Indians in ceremonial attire or dressed for battle are
those of a people who used personal decoration lavishly and in great
variety. We now catch a glimpse of so-called primitive peoples by
means of color photography and the ingenuity of styles and the
profusion of the use of ornament on the body, especially on the
head and neck, is both startling and thought-provoking. In general
the man is more flamboyantly befeathered, painted, tattooed, and
decorated with beads than the woman and this is more in accord
with the animal world, where the male is more attractively endowed with color than the female. Could it be that one of the
reasons for man's preoccupation with the decoration of his body is a
sense of inadequacy as a naked creature? Birds have brilliant
feathers, animals have glossy pelts, and these feathers and furs exist
in abundance and are distinctive of a great variety of species. But
man, who more than any other animal orients himself by means of
sight rather than by smell or touch, finds himself, as the heir of
Adam and Eve, susceptible to observation and to a kind of aesthetic
shame. He stands erect and naked, exposed on every side, and is,
according to Mark Twain, the only animal that blushes.

It would follow, then, that to alleviate this sense of inadequacy he has taken the admired feathers and put them in his hair,
strung them around his neck, hung them from his ears, and made
them into brilliant capes to throw over his shoulders. He has worn
pelts around shoulders and loins, strung teeth, claws, and tusks
about his neck or from his ears. Tattooing and welting have been
practiced by people especially in areas where clothing is undesirable
due to intense heat, and this is justified by them as a means of making their human bodies more like those of the animals with which
they share their habitat. The Bushmen of South Africa still undergo
the welting procedure today and state explicitly why they do so.

"She had her row of scars—though, delicate and arching over

her brow, making her eyes seem wider; as well as a row of striped scars along her thighs. These, say Bushmen, are made to imitate the beauty of zebras, and many women wear them, having been decorated when they were still young. It is a painful procedure. The cuts are made on the thighs and forehead with a knife or ax blade, then charcoal is rubbed in, but the woman told us later that in her case, it had been worth the pain and trouble because, she said, she was extremely ugly and had been made more beautiful."*

The striped effect of the strands of ostrich-egg-shell beads which the same Bushmen painstakingly make and wear in quantity also avowedly serves to make them look more like the admired zebra. The Sonjo, too, paint their bodies to resemble this striped animal with which they live, and which they consider handsome.

We need not look back to primitive peoples of the past, nor sideward to the so-called primitive cultures of today, to see what has resulted from this ardent admiration for animals. Among the greatest luxuries of the present day are feathers and furs, and the demand for them is so great that only the intervention of governments save many of our most colorful birds, like the egret and the ostrich, and animals such as the seal and the otter from total extinction.

There are other functions of decoration than that of merely emulating the more colorful and designed animals. Ornament has been used to differentiate one tribe from another, one people from another. Any American child can tell the difference between a Sioux feather war bonnet and the Mohawk hair cut and feather headdress. These tribes did not happen to be neighbors, but it has been of great importance to man to know his own people and his enemy at a glance at some distance as well as in the excitement of battle. Thus one finds an astonishing variety of ornamentation of heads and faces to make people recognizable as members of their own group and unmistakably unlike their neighbors.

Within the tribe too there must be differentiation. Rank must

* Elizabeth M. Thomas, *The Harmless People*

be visibly defined. The headdress or necklace of the headman or chief gives him pre-eminence in a group and becomes the symbol of his office. The lesser chiefs, too, must indicate their powerful positions visibly and the women of their households partake of their extra privileges of adornment. Medicine men also wear some of their paraphernalia around their necks and arms and are thus defined within the hierarchy of power and of magic influence in their tribe.

The Egyptian nobility wore their broad collars of faience beads; European royalty, long necklaces of pearls and precious stones; the rajahs of India their rubies and gold; the Aztec princes their jade beads. These were privileged people. They not only commanded the wealth to purchase such costly finery, but the right to wear it was theirs by royal edict and this prerogative was jealously guarded. Now beads are in the open market and mass production makes them available to almost anyone. But there are still some designations of status and rank which can only legitimately be worn by those entitled to them—crowns, chains of office, membership pins and symbols, and, of course, the wedding ring. Modern men, dressed in their severely plain business or working clothes, may consider ornamentation effeminate in general, but even they wear jeweled military decorations with pride, these being unchallengeably masculine.

In addition to their power as distinguishing ornament, however, we must assume that beads have always been regarded as eye-catching and charming, therefore enhancing the wearer. Even the oldest and crudest beads which archeologists have unearthed from ancient graves give some indication of their past charm. They are formed with care in round, cylindrical, or oblong shapes, smoothed and polished to a high degree of finish, and often have a suggestion still of the color or luster which made them attractive and valuable to their owners. But scarcity, which usually adds value to materials, has not been the main factor guiding the bead craftsman in selecting what he would use for his purposes. There are many valuable materials which have never been used as far as we know because they are dull, rough, and colorless. Brightly colored seeds are universal favorites for piercing and stringing. Smoothly polished bone and ivory, tortoise shell, and porcupine quills have been fashioned into objects which can be strung and worn—materials which have a definite claim to beauty in themselves, and which are enhanced by grouping and arranging with contrasting colors and textures.

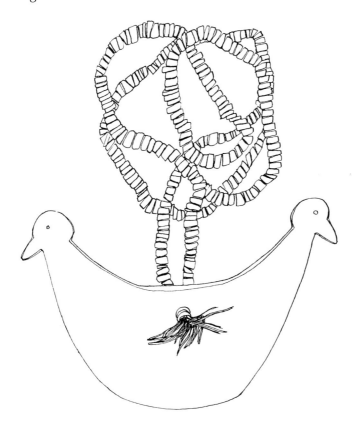

Rough coral beads with pearl-shell ornament

The great variety and luster of shells has made them one of the most sought-after materials by bead craftsmen. Coral, amber, pearls, and the softer stones such as turquoise are the very sources of our names for color. When glass was invented, making the reproduction of all these natural products possible, and when techniques were developed to make it clear, bright, transparent, and sparkling in its own right, man's delight in it was expressed by the enormous demands he made on the glassmakers. Beads made of simple or inexpensive materials are obviously worn for pleasure, and if, as some social philosophers would have us believe, beads are only symbols of power and prestige, is it not thought-provoking that man expresses even these needs with colorful, bright, eye-satisfying objects?

But these aesthetic qualities and the gratifications of self-adornment could probably not alone account for the power beads have exercised in the world. In order to understand this power, certain other more practical characteristics should be taken into account.

Beads can be strung. This makes it possible to wear them around the neck, to tie strings of them around legs, arms, and waist, and to decorate clothing with them. Thus they are easy for the individual to transport, and where they represent his wealth they are easier to keep track of than flocks of sheep or cattle. Small, valuable articles have always been the most satisfactory for use in trade. Even a camel could transport large quantities of beads, and when boats were small, beads and bells were an ideal cargo, as Columbus well knew.

Beads are also durable as well as small, and durable, compact objects are those which remain longest in circulation. A visit to any of our museums of ancient works of art tells the same story. The large objects, however marvelous, are seldom whole. Time has been rough with them and only with an effort of the imagination can one see how they may once have appeared. Wind and weather do their work and men themselves despoil and destroy. However, the perfectly preserved small objects, carved symbols, amulets, and beads which were buried with their owners can now still speak with undiminished clarity of those who wore them, of the craftsmen who fashioned them, and of the society in which such art flourished.

Carved ornaments of Pre-Columbian jade

Durability also makes inheritance possible. Old beads are those most valued in many parts of the world. The people of Borneo who prize their old beads so highly are said to consider those beads best which have an "unimpeachable ancestral genealogy." The Ashanti in Africa have through generations treasured the multi-colored glass beads which were probably made in Mesopotamia or Egypt in ancient times, and the oblong brown bead with white markings found in Tibet, and discussed earlier, only increases in value and magic power with age. Beads of metal have only endured when safely buried, because metal lends itself to melting down into new forms—mostly money—and so the craftsman's work is sacrificed to immediate urgencies. This was largely the fate of the marvelous gold jewelry from Mexico, of which Dürer wrote in 1519 when it was displayed in Brussels:

"Also did I see the things which one brought to the king from the new golden land. . . . And I have seen nothing in all my live long days which so filled my heart with joy as these things. When I saw there wondrous artful things and I was astounded at the subtle genius of the people in foreign lands. And I know not how to relate all the things which I beheld there."*

* W. W. Kertesz, *Historia Universal de las Joyas*

Since Albrecht Dürer had studied with a goldsmith in his youth and could therefore judge this treasure with an expert eye, it is our loss that he knew "not how to relate all the things" he beheld there.

Aztec bell

Beads, made out of such a wide range of materials, offer an equally wide range of difficulties to the craftsman who designs and forms them. It must have required skill, hours of patient concentration and hard work, to form the earliest stone bead and then to pierce it from both sides so that the perforations would meet in the middle. Making wampum out of sea shells or grinding down strings of ostrich-egg-shell disks is time-consuming labor. The shell disks are delicate, although they do protect one another once they are strung, and this slow, tedious work is for the evening campfires when the necessities of the day have been taken care of. But when men first formed beads out of clay and colored them with dyes, or out of faience and fired them, and when they finally learned to make glass beads, they were really in business. For beads manufactured by these methods could be produced in such quantities that a world market might be supplied. It was and still is.

Another attribute of the bead is its usefulness as a counting device which can be carried on the person and manipulated where needed. In Chinese stores the world over one can still see in use the box with wire-strung beads which the shopkeeper deftly moves with his fingers in order to compute the price accurately and visibly. The abacus is also widely used in Russia even today. It was for this

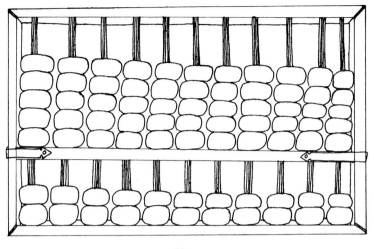

Abacus

practical reason that beads became acceptable to that powerful patron, the Church, in the form of rosaries. During the Middle Ages, when the wearing of jewelry as mere playful adornment was frowned on by the clergy as being frivolous and vain, the bead found a sanctified acceptance, and from this usage we have in fact derived the very word for our subject: for our English word "bead" has come down through the years from the same source as the German word *beten* meaning "to pray," and literally means "prayer" or, as in older English texts, "bede." The rosary, however, was adopted by the Catholic Church rather late in its history (366) and apparently was first mentioned by St. Augustine. The intention in its use was of course that no prayer should be omitted. It was, therefore, truly a counting device, probably incorporated in church ritual in acceptance of an ancient religious pattern, for throughout Asia and the Orient beads have been used as a way of "telling prayers." Marco Polo relates how, between Malabar and Zeilan "where they fish for pearls," "the king has a silken thread around his neck with 104 faire pearles as beads to number his prayers, of which he must daily say so many to his idols." And Captain Hawkins, another great traveler, gives us this description of the great Mogul of Agra: "At break of day at his devotions he has 8 chains of beads, 400 in each chain, formed of all kinds of precious stones; he turneth over his beads and saith 3200 words, and then his prayer is ended."*

Throughout India, China, and Japan, rosaries have been and are used by Buddhists and Mohammedans, and they are fashioned of all kinds of materials from precious stones to string. The beads are not strung into the same groupings as those in the Catholic rosary, but the rosary is used in a similar manner to insure the devout that no prayer has been omitted.

There is another short strand of loosely strung beads somewhat resembling a rosary which is frequently seen in Greece and Turkey. The beads are smooth and light—amber is a preferred material—and men simply handle them for the pleasure of the tactile sensation, and as a calming activity. In railway stations and airports, in cafes and parks, men—never women—may be observed at this diversion, the owners of these beads keeping them always at hand, and this is the justification for referring to them as "worry beads." The Chinese people too have kept beads and polished objects, especially jade, in the pocket to be fondled by the hand. Blind children especially enjoy tactile activity with beads, and thus can at least join in the sensory pleasure which people have always found in the touch of smooth, rounded surfaces.

Beads have also represented wealth—wealth that can be stored and hidden as well as carried on the person. So the Navajo wears his turquoise wealth and the African native his nearly priceless aggri beads. And so the ancient kings of the Western world accumulated their treasure—the jewels which could dazzle their subjects on ceremonial occasions, could serve as ransom if they were unfortunate enough to become captives, or could be sold if money was

* Marian Wallace-Dunlap, *Glass in the Old World*

Rosary

needed to pursue a war. Today, no less, precious stones and pearls represent safely invested assets.

But wealth and currency usually take different forms. Wealth can consist of many and varied things, such as water buffalo or the tremendous Yap Island stones, but useful currency should present a uniform and easily recognizable appearance, countable and durable, of a material which is limited in quantity. Stone beads have been used as currency—notably jade in Chile, long cylindrical stone forms in early California, carnelian in the Pelem Islands and in parts of East Africa. Glass beads have also served as currency where the market did not become flooded by too-hasty importation from manufacturing centers. But the material out of which currency has been made most universally is shell.

We think immediately of wampum when shell money is mentioned, but this term is now rather loosely used. Real wampum is almost never to be seen outside of museums.

The Indians of North America were by no means unique in their predilection for shell as the material out of which to make bead money. Shells have been used for ornament and for currency by a great proportion of the peoples of the world; in fact they may be regarded both as the most valued of personal ornaments and the most ornamental form of money. Small shell disks, pierced and strung and looking like wampum cylinders, olive shells strung through a single hole and separated by knots, cowrie shells pierced at both ends and stitched into patterns or even woven into fabric itself—whatever the method used, they were wearable and countable, but unlike the standardized coin of today their value increased commercially if the designed ornament was aesthetically pleasing.

Natives in the center of South America and on the North American continent, the prehistoric peoples of Europe, the people of Africa and the South Seas have all used shell beads for money. No satisfactory explanation has been found for this parallel phenomenon since the areas involved are so remote from one another that the practice must have developed independently. But from the evidence all over the world it is clear that human beings have this in common: they have found certain materials attractive to eye and touch and have sought to increase the color, light, and texture by heightened polish in order to form and design ornaments which have then been displayed on their bodies. The universality of the desire for shell ornamentation added to the other qualifications of countability, durability, and availability made it a natural currency.

Where sea shells and fresh-water shells have not been available, egg shell has been used, notably ostrich-egg shells in South Africa. In the South Seas shell money made of deep-sea shell is more highly prized than that of shells more easily available near the shore. In Africa the cowrie is worth more inland and in the west than on the east coast where it is more common. But everywhere, with primitive tools, the labor of forming and piercing the shell is an arduous and painstaking procedure often accompanied by magic and shrouded in secrecy, and the province of specially delegated craftsmen. The insuring of a special aura of procedure in this way also, of course, serves as an anti-inflation measure.

The evidence that the use of beads and shell ornaments for currency is widespread is provided by the accounts of travelers. In the past those travelers who kept detailed records were often merchants like Marco Polo who combined exploration and adventure with an eye to business. Today anthropologists record painstakingly what they learn about the past and present of non-Western peoples. They visit South America, Africa, and the South Seas, noting present-day transactions involving money of whatever kind and regularly report that previously in these areas beads and shells were used as currency. Early documents recording the observations of travelers note, for example, that "small red glass beads made in the Kingdom of Cambay" were currency in the mountainous country due west of Zanzibar in 1500 and in Timbuctoo at about that time "in matters of small value they use certain shells brought hither out of the Kingdom of Persia." In Nigeria two merchants from London note in 1589, "Their money is pretie white shells, for golde and silver we saw none." Somewhat later Michael Angelo Denis de Carli, in *A curious and exact account of a Voyage to Congo in the years 1666–67*, gives us the following information: shells, "for which all things are to be bought as if they were money," are eagerly sought after and bartered for by the natives because with them they can trade with inland people "who adore the sea and call these shells, which their country does not afford, 'God's children,' for which reason they look upon them as a treasure and take them in exchange for any sort of goods they have. Among them he is richest and happiest who has most of them." We are also informed, in corroboration of the assumption that the cowrie shell was in general use as currency, that the first postage stamps printed by the mission press in Uganda were set up in denominations of five or ten cowries.

If the detail and liveliness of the recording of these facts by travelers suggest a trace of surprise it is indeed understandable. To find in isolated areas of mid-Africa and in the center of South America natives whose most cherished possessions are sea shells is astonishing. Their value could, of course, be considered a virtue of their uniqueness, the wonder being how they accomplished the long and complicated journey from the shores of the ocean to dense inland forests. They were rare in central Africa and still are in the uncharted country in mid South America. But they are not rare in the South Seas, where they have nevertheless served as acceptable currency for hundreds of years.

Travelers and anthropologists have noted the various methods of drilling and stringing the shells and the types of shells used predominantly. These descriptions are methodical and carefully detailed, suggesting the attention given to an expected phenomenon. A trace of an element of surprise is detected only in instances where beads have been found to rate higher in value than shells. "Trade is carried on by barter, the most prized article of exchange being a species of bead, by no means plentiful, called by them lakkai, of an ochreous red color, evidently some sort of soft stone. Whence these beads come is quite unknown, and no imitation yet made in Birmingham or elsewhere has been sufficiently exact to deceive the native."*

That beads were used in North America for trade with the Indians is common knowledge; how they were used as barter goods

* Henry O. Forbes, *A Naturalist's Wanderings in the Eastern Archipelago*

in the African slave trade has also been described. But in a historical sense this trade, although it was carried on for a few hundred years, seems short-lived compared to the duration of the reign of shells as the acceptable currency of the world.

And so beads in their many forms have played their many roles.

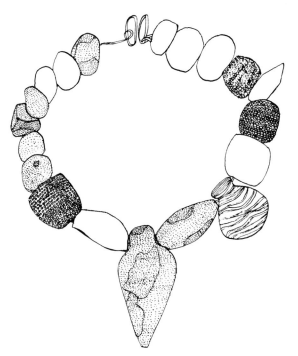

Ancient Egyptian necklace

If man felt his upright and naked body too exposed, too undifferentiated in contrast with the more defined and handsomely endowed animal species of his world, he found ways out of his dilemma, turning a weakness into a strength. Since he was free to choose, his intelligence was challenged, his imagination stimulated, and he observed and made inventive use of the materials offered by his environment. He could paint his body yellow or red, welt it or wear strings of white shell beads to make it look striped, devise an array of decorations to make himself fearsome for battle and festive for dance ceremonials. His clothing and his personal decoration became the product of his own aesthetic expression and the outward and visible mark of his identity.

In summary, then, it is apparent that this small object, the bead, fits singularly well into a number of human endeavors. Man needs to feel special in the sense that he belongs to "*the* people" (as so many tribes have called themselves) and special because of the hierarchies within social organization. Much of this differentiation can be made visible by personal decoration or insignia which must be rare and durable and magically sanctioned. Distinctive ornamentation also satisfies man's need for aesthetic pleasure. His eye sees and fastens on the bright object, he gathers it in, makes it his, treasures it, and then enjoys wearing it. Furthermore, some of the playfulness which he preserves from his childhood (a long childhood is also universal) gives him satisfaction in stringing and arranging his collection of shells, seeds, or stones and in varying patterns, in adding to or rearranging it. The final form of the decorative object, a playfully devised rattle of seeds or a macabre ornament of brilliant beetle backs dangling from a shrunken head, may be startling but it is also certainly a uniquely human creation.

And human beings worry. They worry about their own competence, they worry about friends and enemies and especially about the ever-present spirits of the dead. They are dependent on the elements for their livelihood, elements over which they have no control. So they look to magic for support and magically powerful objects that you can carry with you are eminently reassuring. Amulets and charms and special kinds of beads thus have been universally endowed with magic properties. And insofar as the confidence placed in them helped their wearers conserve their energies to face defined emergencies rather than to live in constant apprehension of imagined ones, they served their owners well.

"Smiling" Figure (Veracruz, Mexico)

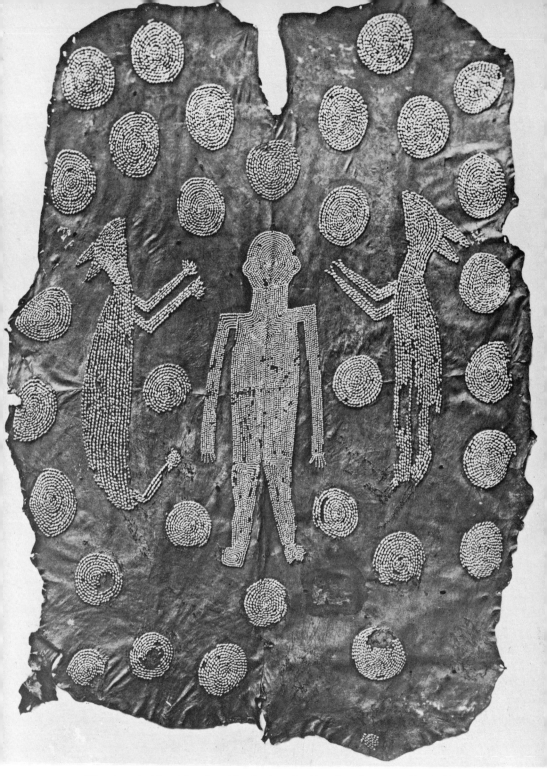

"Powhatan's Mantle"—deerskin cloak embroidered with marginella shells

Woman's Dress—deerskin, porcupine quills, beads
(Saskatchewan, Canada; Cree)

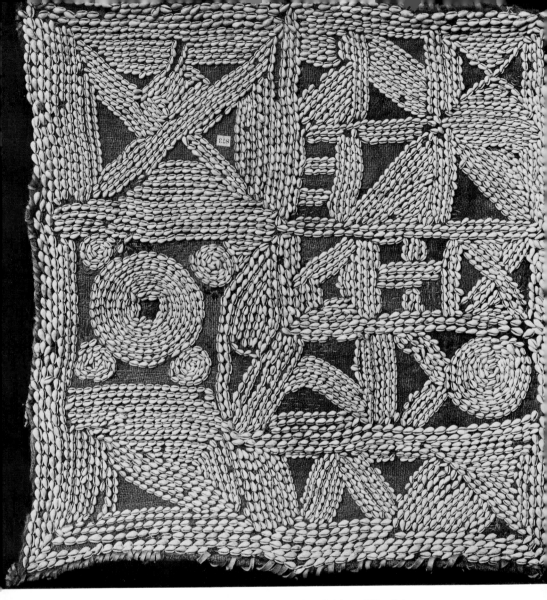

Marginella shell embroidered fabric (Florida)

Opposite page, *Maya Figures (Campeche, Mexico)*

Bag—buffalo hide (North American Indian)

Chippewa Delegates from White Earth Reservation, Minnesota, to Washington, D.C., 1911

*Necklace—turquoise, coral, ancient dark brown and white beads
of unknown origin*

III

Materials, Craftsmanship, and Manufacture

IT SEEMS TO BE characteristic, perhaps even instinctive, for human beings to collect and string together similar objects. The process itself gives pleasure and may be repeated with variations and additions. Men have always scanned their natural environment to find appropriate objects for collecting and stringing.

Probably the first beads were made of seeds and berries, corn kernels and nuts, since these can be most easily pierced and strung with only a sharp stick or bone for a tool. Primitive peoples of today still use these materials for personal decoration, and indeed our sophisticated modern shops display necklaces of seed beads in colorful masses. But berries belong to the delights of the moment, like all perishable things, and seeds, too, dry up and disintegrate or lose their colors.

Seeds

Early in time, however, men picked up and tied to their persons the stones with naturally formed holes—then as now a lucky find, on beaches or in stream beds. Museums display specimens found in graves—for stone endures—and label them simply "prehistoric." The rock collectors of today also treasure in their collections a few pieces of stone or ossified shell in which somehow a natural hole is formed.

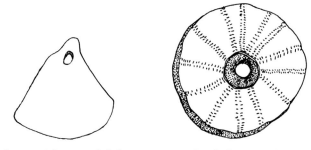

Stone with natural hole   *Ossified sea urchin*

Everywhere in the world, then, men have selected bizarre things for the purpose of piercing and stringing such as shiny beetles' legs, or brown, spicy-smelling cloves, as well as the naturally formed and obviously suitable nuts and berries and seeds. Often when looked at by themselves these elements offer little promise of any extraordinary claim to beauty. A single clove or a beetle's leg does not readily recommend itself as decorative material. But they can be most effectively strung and grouped in a necklace, the repetition resulting in a form and texture which provide an aesthetic pleasure enhanced by the very charm of the unexpected.

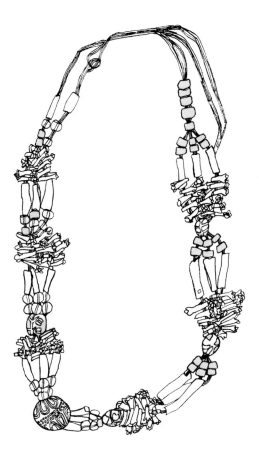

Necklace of coral, cloves, and glass beads

Porcupine quills, which lend themselves to the embroidering of geometric patterns on tanned hide, have also been dyed and strung as long cylindrical beads. The islanders in southern waters use the shell of the tortoise as a material out of which ornaments can be fashioned although the process of carving and polishing requires patience and skill. In India certain grasses were used to form beads, the "golden grass" providing a finished sphere so glowing in texture and so deftly made that, except for their extreme lightness, one would certainly assume these beads to be fashioned of metal. The iridescent green backs of beetles have also been used as decorative material for stringing, and small wonder, for when massed the color is vivid, the ornament handsome.

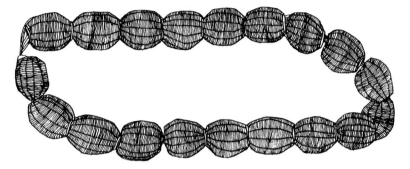

Beads formed of "golden grass" from India

Perhaps it is less surprising that teeth have suggested themselves rather universally as elements out of which necklaces can be made. After all, they exist in their natural state in a curved row and are shiningly displayed in both snarling and smiling settings. A necklace made of a hundred and fifty human incisors was found in the Gilbert Islands and dated as having been worn in 2900 B.C. Dogs' teeth are also collected and worn in the South Seas by the Mauris and other tribes, and the teeth of lions and tigers are highly prized in Africa, for the finished necklace looks both fierce and awe-inspiring. The claws of wild animals equally suggest themselves for stringing while in addition proclaiming the prowess of the wearer as a hunter and magically endowing him with the courage and skill of his erstwhile prey. Similarly, snake vertebrae and rattlesnake tails, human knuckle bones, and hollow-stemmed grasses have been arranged and strung as ornaments. The Eskimos, in turn, have found in the tusks of the walrus a material which can be carved into decorative forms, and the tusk of the elephant has been an ardently desired and sought-after "natural" substance out of which to make beads and ornaments.

A comprehensive list of bead materials, then, would be long and full of the unexpected. However, there are a few universally acclaimed materials the names of which conjure up the almost mythical qualities which have become associated with them: shells, pearls, amber, turquoise, and jade.

Early stone beads

It is difficult to imagine a time when man was unobservant of *shells*. They contain food, and their forms provide a variety of tools, containers, scoops, ladles; their sharp edges cut, and pointed slivers may be used for piercing and sewing and for fish hooks. Their usefulness as currency has already been described.

But a shell was and is more than all these things. Perhaps only a poet could find words to describe the astounding variety of structure, form, and color found in these strange marine dwelling places. Men have marveled at their perfection—and regarded them with some superstitious awe.

Land-snail shells

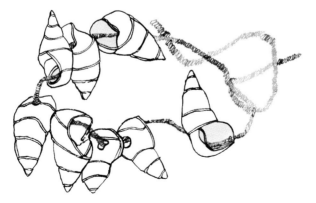

An ancient necklace of crudely cut emeralds from Ceylon may include two or three shells. Trade beads of carnelian and bone from East Africa are sometimes strung with a small cluster of shells. Turquoise beads from the American Southwest are often interspersed with pieces of coral-colored shell from the distant Pacific coast and the iridescent abalone shell has been carved into ornamental forms and figures to be suspended from neck or ear. Shells are fascinating in their own right but a survey of how man has devised ways of using them for his aesthetic pleasure could provide impressive insight into human creativity.

One of the least prepossessing of the shell family from the point of view of color and form is the oyster. It has a rough, gray, uneven shell which when opened proves to contain a rather slippery mass of grayish white tissue, which is both nutritious and delicious if unlovely. But once in a while, once in a thousand such openings, a lustrous, perfect sphere of a soft iridescent color is found lodged inside the shell—a *pearl*. Surrounded with the aura of chance and the mystery of perfection, it is a gift from the sea, already formed and glowing with a sovereign loveliness which human craftsmanship cannot duplicate or enhance.

The German word for bead is *"perle"* and it is usually modified by a word which indicates the material out of which it is made —*Glasperle, Bernsteinperle* (amber), *Korallenperle* (coral). This usage only does due homage to the most perfect bead which nature has provided, for the pearl has all the attributes of the bead par excellence—it is, as it were, the essence of bead.

Not all pearls, of course, are perfect spheres. There are button pearls—rather flat at the top and bottom, pear-shaped pearls, and baroque pearls, which may occur in a great variety of forms. The beauty of the pearl, in fact, with its soft evening-sky tints and the glow of water which it seems to have caught and held is shared by shells, but shells are fragile. The pearl not only exists in an extraordinary range of colors—rose, gray, blue, gold, green, steel gray, and creamy white and these colors iridescent and elusive—but it is durable and remains unspoiled by use and time. It is also not too difficult to pierce, being in substance a form of shell. The pearl thus has three of the main attributes of the ideal bead: durability, workability, and rarity, as well as flawless beauty; no wonder that it has been valued as "of great price" since time immemorial.

It also suggests itself to mythological symbolism. The pearl is regarded as representing the essence of purity, the feminine principle, the moon. Part of the mystery which surrounds it lies in its unpredictable occurrence. The Greeks offered the suggestion that pearl-bearing shells had been struck by lightning. Other explanations conclude that pearls are the tears of the oyster or even the crystallized tears of angels. A traveler to India in 1159 offers us from El Cathif the following information:

"In this vicinity the pearls are found: about the twenty-fourth of the month of Nidan [April] large drops of rain are observed upon the surface of the water, which are swallowed by the reptiles, after this they close their shells and fall upon the bottom of the sea; about the middle of the month of Thishri [October], some people dive with the assistance of ropes, collect these reptiles from the bottom and bring them up with them, after which they are opened and the pearls taken out."[*]

Actually, the organic cause of the formation of the pearl was only clarified in the early years of the twentieth century, and we now know that the growth of this perfect object is the reaction of the system of the oyster to imperfection, to disturbance. When a perhaps minute foreign body such as a grain of sand or a particle of silt or even a tiny flatworm penetrates the shell into the body of the oyster, pearl-secreting cells form a sac to cover the irritating substance with nacre. As long as the oyster lives, which may be for twenty years, it continues to produce the nacre and thus to increase the size of the pearl.

[*] R. H. Major, *India in the Fifteenth Century*

Pearl diving is an ancient trade. The diver must hold his breath while descending on a rope held taut by a stone and go down to a depth of thirty or forty feet to find the shells. These he quickly places in a basket and, with the help of his partner in the boat above, he resurfaces, empties his basket, and rests momentarily before going down again. Only one shell in a thousand produces a pearl, and fishing is possible during only a few months of the year. The strain on the diver's lungs is tremendous and sharks are a hazard in the southern waters where the richest oyster beds occur, so it is not surprising to hear that divers lead short lives.

The perfect pearl, however, has a special place among the prized possessions of the Western world. Today we often look with disapproval on conspicuous display of ornament and wealth. But the pearl, true or false, is the bead above criticism. Suitable for the young or the old, in quantity or singly, it reigns unchallenged. Unfortunately, when strung monotonously it also takes on something of the quality of stylized uniformity, but if we must have conspicuous conformity we may be grateful that the pearl is selected for this honor.

AND *amber* was discovered, a link not to the moon, but to the sun.

If one could explain the fascination which amber has had for men since prehistoric times it could help us to better understand some of his deepest yearnings.

Amber exists in a wide range of colors from transparent golden yellow—honey color—to reddish dark brown and almost black. It was originally a sap exuded from a type of pine tree (pinus succinatus) which grew perhaps forty to sixty million years ago on a formerly existing promontory south of present-day Sweden. Since it is light, it was rolled about in the sea after it hardened and finally quantities were deposited in the sands along the coast of Samland in East Prussia. In this slowly hardened sap it is sometimes possible to find small insects such as ants, gnats, spiders, and silverfish that have been imprisoned and preserved. Such pieces of amber were especially treasured in the past and are among the most interesting specimens in our museums today.

Since amber becomes electrically charged when rubbed, so that small bits of dust and lint will adhere to it, mystical properties have also been attributed to it. The Greeks called it "electra." But it was for its brilliance and color as well as for this strange characteristic that it was admired and considered to be the essence of the rays of the sun, congealed in the sea and then cast up on the shore. In the Odyssey we read:

> Eurymachus
> Received a golden necklace, richly wrought,
> and set with amber beads, that glowed as if
> with sunshine.

Amber with naturally formed hole

While amber played its historical role as a valued gem largely in Europe, *jade* has had high and ancient prestige in three large areas of the world. In China it was used as burial treasure in prehistoric times, and has maintained its pre-eminence as a jewel up to the present day. In aboriginal Australia and New Zealand ornaments of jade—green stones—were precious possessions. In Central America, the Mayans and Aztecs held jade in highest regard, wearing beads and inlaid ornaments of this stone, treasuring it above all things, and Cortez was understandably surprised when he was offered pieces of jade by the Aztecs with the assurance that they were more valuable than the gold for which he was searching.

The word jade is used to describe two minerals—nephrite and jadeite—which actually have a different composition and structure but which look so much alike in color and substance that they cannot always be easily distinguished from one another.

The nephrites are admired for their interesting mottling, which may suggest the form that the carver will follow in his designing. The jadeites are more translucent and lustrous, more vivid, and can be polished to a glassy sheen.

In China the source of jade is thought to have been the distant and almost inaccessible regions of Sinkiang (Chinese Turkestan). It is found high in the mountains above the snow line and was transported by a long and arduous trade-route journey which involved as much as six months of travel. One method of obtaining it was to light fires around the larger stones, called "mountain material," in order to crack them. The pieces were then thrown down the mountainside to the valleys below, there to be gathered. Other pieces were found in the valley streams in the form of pebbles, called seed jade. Later, in the eighteenth century and afterward, the chief source of jadeite was Burma. It was shipped by river to Rangoon and then by sea to the Chinese ports, Canton, Shanghai, and Hong Kong.

Jade is varied and subtle in color: it ranges from white, gray, cream, yellow, and brown to black, and through every conceivable tone of green—apple green, grass green, sea green, to darker shades of spinach and seaweed. At the same time it is a very hard stone and was useful to men in prehistoric times as a material out of which tools and even weapons could be made. No wonder that the Chinese as well as the Mayans and Aztecs of Central America came to invest a material of such varied appearance and uses with supernatural power, which gave it importance and prestige beyond its practical usefulness.

The Chinese, in fact, thought of it as having even a supernatural origin, and used it in religious ceremonies as a means of attaining contact with the powers which control the universe and govern the movements of the sun, moon, and stars, and to mediate between men and the gods of the mountains, the waters and the elements.

Jade beads have been found in the earliest Chou burials dating as early as 1122 B.C. Ornaments made of jade were worn by the great officers. The Li Chi tells us that when so adorned they "raised their toes and trailed their heels" and considered "their jade tokens as insignia of rank." And jade, unlike other important stones, was also appreciated for its sonorous qualities. The emperor, we are told, wore a cap with twelve pendants of jade beads on strings suspended from it, and these might vary in color at different seasons of the year. The Son of Heaven "when advancing inclined forward a little; he held himself up straight and in all these movements the pieces of jade emitted their tinklings—so also the man of rank when in his carriage heard the harmonious sound of its bells, and when walking those of his pendant jade stones, and in this way evil and depraved throughts found no entrance in his mind."*

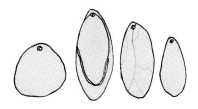

Jade pendants

Confucius summarized the meaning of jade in one statement. On being asked why the superior man preferred jade to soapstone, he is said to have replied (so R. S. Jenyns reports): "It is not because the soapstone is plentiful and because jade is rare that he sets so high a value upon it. Anciently superior men found the likeness of all excellent qualities in jade. Soft and smooth and glossy it

* R. S. Jenyns, *Chinese Archaic Jades in the British Museum*

appeared to them like benevolence: fine, compact and strong—like intelligence: angular but not sharp cutting—like righteousness: hanging down [in beads] as if it would fall to the ground—like [the humility of] propriety: when struck yielding a note, clear and prolonged, yet terminating abruptly—like music: its flaws not concealing its beauty, nor its beauty concealing its flaws—like loyalty: with an internal radiance issuing from it on every side like good faith; bright as a brilliant rainbow—like heaven: exquisite and in the hills and streams—like the earth: standing out conspicuous as a symbol of rank—like virtue: esteemed by all under the sun— like the path of truth and duty . . . that is why superior man esteems it so highly."

How this hard stone was cut and polished in ancient times is still unknown. There is some evidence from excavations in China that as early as Shang-Yin times (eleventh century B.C.) a rotary knife was used for sawing, fine sand as the indispensable abrasive, and a pointed tool as a drill. The Pre-Columbian beads from middle America show clearly that they have been drilled from both sides, the meeting point in the middle being often no larger than the point of a pin. Considering the crudeness of the then available tools, the craftsman of today can observe the intricacy of the carving of pendants and stones only with envy and admiration.

The source of jade in Central America is unknown. It has been assumed, however, that there must have been indigenous jade which was quarried earlier and was already exhausted by the time of the Spanish conquest. But then some jade may have been imported to Central America in ancient times.

Students of the migration of peoples have suggested that the people who settled in Central America and developed the Mayan and Aztec civilizations may have come from Asia across the Bering Straits. This is a disputed theory, but by whatever route the Orient may have influenced this continent there is no question that the works of art, sculpture, and design of Central America suggest this origin. At any rate, it is tempting to entertain the idea that centuries ago, through their long trek by land or sea to the middle of a distant continent, the Asian ancestors of the Mayans and Aztecs may have carried some of their most cherished ceremonial jade objects with them and then maintained their veneration for this stone by means of which continued intercourse with their gods was possible, and with it a link to the culture which they had left behind them.

Turquoise, the "stone that stole its color from the sky," has been found only in the barren, arid areas of the world, the important productive deposits being in Persia, Central Asia, and the Southwest of the United States. No contact between these cultures is known or even surmised. In a limited quantity, turquoise has also been found in Abyssinia, Nubia, and the Sinai Peninsula. This latter source was known to the Egyptians and exploited by them three thousand years ago. Although turquoise is now considered only semiprecious, there are people even today for whom it is the gem stone of greatest worth: the Arab Bedouins, Tibetans, Mongolians, and the Navajos.

In Egypt the earliest prehistoric graves have yielded beads of turquoise and in the royal tombs at Abydos; among the most important finds were four exceptionally fine bracelets made of gold, amethyst, and turquoise beads. The earliest historical allusions to turquoise have been found in Egyptian inscriptions, which give evidence that it was mined in the Sinai Peninsula from before the first and up to the Twentieth Dynasty. In the remains of the mines at Serabit and El Khadem on Sinai, there are many inscriptions and carvings commemorating Hathor, the cow goddess, "divinity of the turquoise lands." In fact, the country as a whole is referred to in these inscriptions as "malkat" or "country of turquoise."

Much of Egyptian faience so closely resembles turquoise in color that it is sometimes difficult to tell them apart at a glance. This is undoubtedly not a chance likeness, for throughout Asia and Egypt the color of turquoise was believed to have potent magical properties. In ancient inscriptions this faience is referred to as "false malkat." In Persia, Nishapur, two hundred twenty-five miles east of the Caspian Sea and close to well-used caravan routes, has long been the most important locality in the world for the production of turquoise. The very name by which the gem is known to the Western world derives from the fact that Nishapur was once considered to be in Turkey, itself very vaguely defined.

There is no conclusive proof of exploitation of the mines in Persia earlier than the tenth century A.D., but that the deposits were worked in about 2100 B.C. is suggested by the name of one of the openings: "Isaac's Mine." Tradition has it that it was discovered by Jacob's father. Also, ruins of Anau in Turkestan, belonging to a cultural period of great antiquity, have yielded turquoise beads as well as tombs of the first to the third century A.D. in the Caucasus.

In Tibet turquoise is regarded as a separate substance in itself, not a stone. There is no exact information concerning its occurrence but the extensive use points to a local supply; also, there is an indigenous word for it, "gyu." Most Tibetan turquoise, however, is of mediocre quality. Usually it is greenish, the larger masses being mottled with black matrix. Here also the deep-blue gems are the most highly valued.

In all places where it is found turquoise is classified according to color (shade and permanence) and hardness and is used in jewelry of all kinds, for both men and women, as well as to decorate their richly ornamented dress. It is also extensively used to decorate holy objects: rosaries, Buddha's eyes, charm boxes, prayer wheels, amulets, altars, holy-water vases, censers, and musical instruments. It will pass for currency in many parts of Tibet.

The Chinese looked upon turquoise as a transformation from the fir tree; their name for it means "green fir-stone." They regarded it more as an ornamental material for inlaying, mosaics, and carving, and put it to much the same use as jade, to which it remained, however, always secondary.

Marco Polo, in his *Travels*, notes the mining of turquoise in the province of Kerman in Persia and Caind (presently Szechuan) in China. It was first introduced into China, probably from Tibet, in the thirteenth or fourteenth century A.D. and its utilization led to the discovery of Chinese mines which were being worked in Marco Polo's time.

From the Middle Ages on turquoise in Europe was classified as "oriental" (blue, from Persia and India) and "occidental" (green, found in Spain, Germany, Bohemia, and Silesia). The so-called green turquoise was in reality copper-colored fossil bone, a fact which was not established until about 1800, and even then not completely accepted. The confusion between the two, and the belief in the transformation of one into the other by means of heat, occurs persistently in the writings of the alchemists.

In the Americas we first hear of turquoise as listed among the presents sent by Montezuma to Cortez, who received a turquoise-encrusted snake mask from the great Aztec king. Later numerous masks of turquoise mosaic were shipped to Europe from Mexico by the Spanish invaders. The Incas of South America also knew and used turquoise and a wealth of turquoise ornaments was found in the excavations of a Pre-Columbian culture in Argentina. In Bolivia and Chile, beads and amulets of this stone have also been found. Yet no American source of turquoise has been discovered outside the Southwest of the United States. Arizona, California, Colorado, Nevada, and New Mexico are the states in which there are known deposits, and in all these areas there are mines which show evidence of prehistoric workings. One must then infer that the turquoise of Mexico and South America was obtained by trade from the Pueblo Indians.

In the hills of Los Carrillas, about twenty miles southeast of Santa Fe, New Mexico, the most famous area of turquoise mining is found; in fact, only turquoise mined from this locality is valued highly enough by many Pueblo Indians to be used for ceremonial purposes. The name for the hills of Los Carrillas is translated variously as "turquoise mountainous place," "place where turquoise is dug," or "turquoise hut."

According to prehistoric finds, the Pueblo used turquoise more extensively than any other groups of Indians. When found in the canyons and rivers it was most commonly fashioned into discoidal and cylindrical beads. A superb necklace of twenty-five hundred beads was found in Pueblo Bonita in Chaco Canyon; in Elden Pueblo turquoise and shell beads were sifted out of the soil near skeletons. When strung, these beads proved to be strands of a necklace several feet in length.

As every traveler knows, the Indians of the Southwest now use turquoise both for the jewelry they wear every day and for the special necklaces and bracelets which are worn for ceremonial purposes, such as dances. It holds a fundamental place in their religious ideas and the ceremonial expression of these ideas, and to them turquoise is as surely of celestial origin as amber and jade were for the peoples who found and used them: the Pueblo named turquoise the stone that stole its color from the sky. It plays an important role in many of their myths, as well as in those of the Hopi and Zuñi:

"In the beginning Hard Being Woman, who owns shells, coral, turquoise and all stones, gave the chief's son a bag filled with beads, among them Turquoises. She warned him not to open the bag until he reached home. Every morning the bag was heavier, but on the fifth night, unable to restrain his curiosity, he opened it. The next morning all that had been added were gone, only the original contents of the bag remained. And that is why the Hopi have so few beads."

"The eagle bore the Zuñi youth upward into the Skyworld, where it alighted with its beloved burden on the summit of the mountain of Turquoises so blue that the lights shining on it painted the sky blue."

Both Hopi and Zuñi wear long turquoise necklaces and double loops of turquoise beads over their ears on ceremonial occasions. Such ceremonial necklaces are handed down from generation to generation. But, as is true with other precious stones, the supernatural attributes of turquoise only enhance its intrinsic value, and so turquoise is said to be the Zuñi savings bank. After the sale of wool in the spring a man liquidates his debts, reclaims his pawned jewelry, and invests any balance in turquoise.

Turquoise disks

It also plays a conspicuous role in Navajo myths and legends. For example:

"The sun was fashioned of a piece of Turquoise, upon which eyes and a mouth had been drawn by means of a crystal dipped in pollen. It gave little light at first, but with the aid of many Turquoises and a lengthy ritual, was made to blaze, and is held up by four poles, two of Turquoise and two of white shell held by twelve men at the cardinal points."

At the present time the turquoise of the Southwest is pretty well mined out and therefore is available only in very small quantities and is of a rather poor quality. But in Santo Domingo Pueblo, where the finest stonecutters work, trade with the Navajo still flourishes. Large quantities of Persian turquoise are being imported from that faraway country and fashioned with modern tools into the traditional Indian discs for the ceremonial necklaces and into stones to be set by the Navajo in silver for eager tourists.

Pearls, as we have said, have always been considered precious, while amber, jade, and turquoise have in our Western world been rated only as semiprecious stones. But even emeralds, rubies, and sapphires, which are among our most precious gems, have all been used in the making of beads. It would seem that only diamonds have resisted transformation into beads, and this probably for two reasons. The diamond is so hard that it would be most difficult to pierce with primitive methods, and since it is sold by weight, it is considered too valuable to pierce. Furthermore, the crystal form to which the diamond owes its great brilliance does not lend itself to being worn with comfort around the neck.

Both precious and semiprecious stones, however, occur in a matrix of less attractive substance. It takes a practiced eye to appraise the latent possibilities of such stones and to judge how they may be improved by polishing. The work of the lapidary is to remove all traces of this matrix, to grind the stone into a pleasing shape, and then to polish it so that no trace of roughness remains and so that the depth of color becomes constant and bright.

As the color and the power of the heavenly bodies and the sky

Old stone beads

are felt to be reflected and contained in rare stones, life-giving heat is thought to glow in *gold*. Man early found gold, the fabulous metal which can be hammered or melted into desired shapes and which never changes color or ceases to shine. It has long been the universal symbol of that which is imperishable, pure, and valuable. The earliest civilizations, the Assyrian, Egyptian, Minoan, Inca, and Mayan, all used gold for making ornaments. It is of little use for other purposes, being too soft for durable tools or firm utensils, but it does have the virtue of being rare and having remained so even after large deposits were found and gold rushes were launched to mine it. It is said that gold was first gathered out of streams like the Indus and the Euphrates by an ingenious method. The pelts of sheep were hung in the flowing water. Gold particles floating downriver adhered to the curly wool and slowly collected so that they could later be brushed or shaken out of the fur. Perhaps this practice gave rise to the legendary image of the Golden Fleece.

Gold has been used extensively for making beads of all shapes and sizes, smooth and textured with wire designs or tiny gold balls, as in granulation. It can be hammered leaf-thin and bent into the desired shape. When heated it becomes molten and may be poured into molds to cool and harden. The goldsmith could thus reproduce in lasting material the natural forms which gave man visual pleasure but which are impermanent and transitory: fruits and flowers, bees, butterflies, and birds and all manner of small insects. He could reproduce in glowing metal the faraway sun, the moon, and the stars, and in this way keep them near and constant. This, too, suggested ceremonial use, sometimes to the exclusion of "monetary value."

The Akan people of the African Gold Coast, one of the richest sources of gold, have venerated it as a sacred representation of the eternal spirit of the sun. Originally, therefore, the greater part of the gold they found was hoarded and used only for ceremonial purposes. In fact, the person who traded his gold was believed to have sold his soul, for his gold, whether in dust, nugget, or granular form, was known as his "soul's gold."

Some of this aura, presumably, has always pervaded man's relationship to gold, and may have contributed to its universal prestige and value throughout the past and up to the present day. If so, there may be additional wisdom in keeping gold reserves well guarded underground, and in allowing people to use only substitutes such as coins of metals that tarnish and green paper bills. If we used the gold itself, perhaps we should all become misers or goldsmiths.

Gold melon beads

The discovery of methods by which metals could be refined and combined led to momentous inventions in the technique of jewelry making. It was equally auspicious when man discovered the properties of *clay*. A small piece may be rolled in the hand and made into a ball or it may be formed on a stick. A sausage-shaped form may be pierced with a stiff reed and when hardened by fire a hole remains where the reed or stick has burned away. To make a bowl, only somewhat longer cylindrical strips wound around on themselves and closed at the edges where they join are necessary. One will never know for sure which idea came first, but a survey of the history of beads and men leads one to conjecture that the bead may have been father to the clay bowl.

Clay beads were certainly made in abundance and first painted and then glazed in patterns very similar to those used on bowls and jars; in fact, some look like miniature jars. Here was a material which was widely available, a skill that could be easily perfected, and an opportunity to design which was limited only by the imagination and skill of the craftsman. The result was a profusion of clay beads, particularly around the Mediterranean Sea, where many have survived for study.

Ceramic bowl beads

With the perfection of the process of glazing, craftsmen made another major discovery. They developed *faience*. This word is derived from the French term for the *"porzellana di Faenza,"* a fine kind of glazed earthenware made in the Italian city of that name. It describes the substance which, as far as we know, is the result of the first successful essay by man in the production of a synthetic material. Just where this was done is still a matter of some speculation. Was it first developed in Mesopotamia or in Egypt, in both of which very early faience objects have been found? Is it possible that the process was discovered simultaneously in both these countries? Scholars say that such a technically ingenious or lucky invention was most unlikely to have occurred simultaneously in two neighboring areas. The answer seems to lie rather in the advanced trade between the two areas, in both of which a high level of civilization had been reached in the skills which satisfy aesthetic needs. At any rate, the first faience was made for personal adornment— beads and small amulets.

The body material of faience is powdered sandy quartz coated with a vitreous glaze to which in earliest Egyptian times (possibly before 4000 B.C.) copper was added. The fired beads which have been found are usually a light blue, which sometimes pales to white or light green with occasional gray-black manganese-colored beads among them. In the Twelfth Dynasty a brilliant turquoise blue was introduced which was used extensively, sometimes with a patterning in black or other colors. These are the beads which we have come to associate with Egypt, with the broad collars represented in Egyptian painting and with those objects in our museums which have been preserved on the mummies of Egyptian nobility, and which we therefore commonly call, somewhat too specifically, "mummy beads."

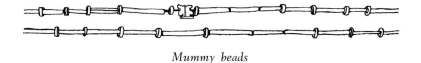

Mummy beads

Glazing was also a process used on stones such as steolite, schist, and quartzite to achieve the greatly admired and desired blue, and many beads and amulets were first delicately carved and formed and then given the final touch of perfection by this heightening of color. Toward the end of the Eighteenth Dynasty (1400 B.C.) polychrome glazes were introduced—violet, red, bright yellow, and apple green with a darker blue and white.

Since beads made of faience were the first to be mass produced, it is perhaps not too surprising that they should have traveled extensively. They were somewhat fragile—especially the long tubular ones—but were, on the other hand, lighter in weight than stone or metal or even clay, and undoubtedly cheaper at the source than other beads. The fact that they developed through stages or fashions in color as well as in form (tubular, segmented, spherical, and barrel-shaped) is an important aid in determining their place of origin and the approximate time of their manufacture.

The spread of faience manufacture was, indeed, remarkable.

In Egypt thousands of molds have been found in the factories at Tel el Amarna which flourished during the Eighteenth and Nineteenth Dynasties. Crete, too, produced faience beads, and a bead factory has been excavated in the workshop area of Knossos. By 1450 B.C. Greece was also involved in the industry, and Syria and possibly India were turning out an ever-increasing volume of beads. The far-ranging expeditions to uncharted lands over sea and land routes which marked the period between 1500 and 1300 B.C. resulted in a dissemination of this product over wide areas of the then known or partially known world. Thus, faience beads dating back to 1400 B.C. have been found in the British Isles. They penetrated as far north as Siberia, and blue and green faience beads have been found on the Lower Volga and the more sophisticated segmented beads on the Upper Tobal east of the Urals. In central East Africa at least one cylindrical faience bead has been unearthed, which also suggests trade from the eastern Mediterranean as early as 1400 B.C.

CONTEMPORARY craftsmen must now rediscover how to make faience beads and how to reproduce the vivid turquoise blue of the ancient Egyptian mummy beads. For this skill was lost, superseded, as it were, by the creation of *glass*, which eventually took over the bulk of bead production in the world and has maintained its supremacy for thousands of years. To the designer it is a material of almost unlimited possibilities for variation in texture, color, and form; for the manufacturer it has the potential of mass production to meet the demands of a growing world market.

There is some divergence of opinion as to where the first glass was made, some authorities believing it to have originated in Ur in Mesopotamia and others in Egypt. Certain it is that the oldest object known to us made wholly of glass is, as we have come to expect, a bead. How the faience workers busy with their glazes discovered that beads could be made without a clay or sand core we will probably never know. But we do know how highly these first glass beads were prized, for we find them used side by side with precious stones in the jewelry of the pharaohs which has been recovered from Egyptian tombs.

If faience beads could be brilliantly colored or varied in form and decorated with designs, glass shared all these attributes and was also less fragile. Above all, it was translucent and thus displayed a depth and variety of color and sparkle which made it a formidable rival of precious stones.

An old story told by Pliny the Elder describes the discovery of glass. A party of Phoenician saltpeter merchants landed by the mouth of the river Belus in Phoenicia (the most northerly coast of present-day Israel). They set about lighting a fire to cook their evening meal. There were no stones on the beach so they made use of some blocks of saltpeter from their cargo on which to rest their kettle. As the fire became very hot the heat fused the sand and saltpeter into a nitreous mass—and thus glass was discovered. Now it is true that the sands of the Belus have been widely used for glassmaking, but otherwise there are several flaws in this account. For one, according to archeological knowledge, glass was made in Egypt and Mesopotamia long before the Phoenicians traded in the Mediterranean. And as already described, glass was used for glazes for hundreds of years before glass beads were produced. And there are questionable points in the story itself. First of all, such a campfire would not reach the degree of heat necessary to fuse the materials involved. Secondly, with the sand mentioned, being composed among other things of calcium carbonate, the necessary ingredient would have been natron (or nitrum), not saltpeter, to produce soda-lime-silicate.

Whatever chance may have led to the initial discovery of glass, no such casual procedures were part of later practices. The making of glass has been a notoriously difficult process. Tremendous quantities of wood were necessary to produce adequate heat, and the control of the heat required exactness. Furthermore, the materials used varied in their chemical composition. The first glass was full of bubbles and not clearly transparent, either because some elements were difficult to eliminate from the materials used or because of the unevenness or low degree of heat. No wonder that one

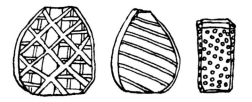

Early pressed-glass beads

could only see "as through a glass darkly." The task of achieving the desired color was also a technical challenge which again exposed the craftsmen to the whims of fickle fortune. The whole procedure being thus full of hazards, it is not surprising that craftsmen of early times resorted to religious ceremony and magic to help them control all these unmanageable elements and to insure the production of satisfactory objects.

Dr. Campbell Thompson has deciphered some Ashurbanipal tablets from Assyria which give us some idea of the complications which magic practices added to the already complex process of glass production.

"When thou settest out the (ground) plan of a furnace for 'minerals,' thou shalt seek out a favourable day in a fortunate month, and thou shalt set out the (ground) plan of the furnace: while they are making the furnace thou shalt watch (them) and shalt work thyself (?). In the house of the furnace thou shalt bring in embryos (born before their time) . . . another (?), a stranger, shall not enter, nor shall one that is unclean tread before them; thou shalt offer the due libations before them; the day when (thou puttest down) the 'mineral' into the furnace thou shalt make a sacrifice before the embryos: thou shalt pour 'kuruuum' over before them.

"Thou shalt kindle a fire underneath the furnace and shalt put down the mineral into the furnace. The men whom thou shalt bring to be over the furnace shall cleanse themselves, and (then) thou let them come down to the furnace."*

No wonder glass was rare and prized!

Considering all the necessary precautions, technical and ceremonial, one can only marvel at the miracle which achieved the variety, color, form, and brilliance of these early glass beads in spite of the vagaries of chance. Or perhaps the challenge of chance is just what is lacking today. Such technical proficiency as has now been developed in the manufacture of glass excludes that certain quality of playful experiment, and this may well be a loss. Once it was the individual craftsman, now it is a team which produces glass, and fancy and imagination, or so it seems, have largely given way to production charts and demand ratings.

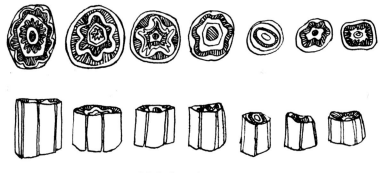

Multifiori glass cones

When glass was first perfected it so much resembled the stones considered precious that it was difficult to distinguish between them. The glassmakers, of course, knew well that if their beads were

* H. C. Beck, *Glass Before 1500 B.C.*

put back into the furnace they would simply melt, whereas the gems survived high temperature without damage. However, most people were understandably reluctant to put valued gems to such a crucial test. Pliny speaks of the extensive trade carried on between the Egyptians and the Indians, the Indians believing the glass stones and beads which they received to be genuine gems, and remarks, "It was the most lucrative trade ever invented by the mind of man."

Earring—glass beads and metal disks

The production of *synthetic stones* was not achieved until the twentieth century, although scientists and alchemists had tried for many centuries to produce them. From a manuscript on the sacred art of alchemy by Olympiodorus of Alexandria in the third century we have this recipe: "Should you wish to make an emerald, take two ounces of fine crystal glass and half an ounce of calcined copper, grind in a mortar, add some alum, melt at an equal fire for three days and nights."*

The synthetic stones of the present day, however, are produced strictly in accord with nature's method of creating these gems. The difference is one of time. Nature unhurriedly takes centuries, allows for rich variations and interesting flaws. Man is able to create the same specific conditions, use identical materials,

* Marion Wallace-Dunlap, *op. cit.*

speed up the process, and produce a stone which only a specialist can distinguish from nature's product.

Perhaps the future holds that everyone will be able to wear and enjoy rubies, sapphires, and emeralds—the jewels of kings—in the quantity and with the exuberance with which glass beads are worn today.

Plastics, too, are now in the bead game. In the markets of faraway Pakistan, plastic beads are combined with brass or gilt reproductions of older bead forms and long strands of plastic amber beads may be seen hanging in the Arabian market stalls in Acre, Israel. And with plastics and synthetics making strides toward increased production and reproduction, probably nothing that we now treasure as rare material for the making of beads will remain very precious as time goes on.

THE SECRET of how to produce *cultured pearls* is also one that was known centuries ago and then apparently lost. The Greeks in the third century A.D. wrote of Arabs who knew how to grow artificial pearls. The Chinese, too, discovered how to insert tiny images of the Buddha into fresh-water clams and to leave them long enough to receive a coating of nacre before retrieving them. These may be seen today at the Museum of Natural History in New York. But only recently the pearl has been reproduced so successfully that a cultured pearl can be bought for a moderate sum. Here also man has studied, understood, and copied nature's own process of creating, and the resulting gem is an amazing achievement, the resulting industry of worldwide importance.

The facts relating to the growth of pearls were discovered by Japanese scientists who devoted many years to experimenting with a variety of procedures, and it was only early in this century that a method for producing spherical pearls was discovered. In the natural pearl the minute foreign body which becomes the nucleus of the pearl is incorporated in the body of the oyster by accident, as it were. The cultured pearl, however, is formed around a core of mother of pearl inserted specifically for this purpose by the pearl grower. The size of the pearl is predetermined by the size of the core inserted and not by the length of time the pearl is allowed to grow. In this way it is possible to grade pearls beforehand, which facilitates the assembling of the necklaces for which they are produced.

The process of inserting the core, however, is a very delicate one and requires skilled technicians. Since it has been determined that the optimal time for pearl growth is a period in the life of the oyster between the ages of three and seven years, three-year-old oysters are selected for the "operation" and are then returned, in cages suspended from rafts, into the sea where they remain undisturbed for from three to five years. The pearls are then harvested, pierced, matched, and strung. In the early 1900's, one of the Japanese scientists, Kokicki Mikimoto, undertook further extensive experiments in how to grow the oysters in quantity under controlled conditions. He established a "pearl farm" on the island of Agowan, invented devices including cages to protect the young oysters, a paint to protect the oyster shell, and a special luster process. Some years later he had eleven such farms and employed more than three thousand persons. There are large numbers of other growers in Japan today and the cultured-pearl industry has become one of great economic importance.

Since it is almost impossible, without a trained eye, to distinguish a fine cultured pearl from one naturally grown, the pearl market has been completely transformed. The price of natural pearls decreased suddenly by 80 per cent in the early 1930's when the Bank of France announced that because of the influx of cultured pearls it could no longer maintain its high credit rates to dealers in Oriental pearls.

THE PRODUCTION of the cultured pearl has been only a further step in the inflation by manufacture, which began with clay, reached its height with glass, and now continues with plastics and synthetic stones. What new materials for beads will the year 2000 bring? With aesthetic appetites only stimulated by the easy influx of synthetics and the possible discovery of how to make gold, what will remain rare, as well as durable, stringable, and aesthetically delightful? Perhaps the moon or the unexplored depths of the sea will become new sources of excitingly new materials. But whatever new may come, the old beads will surely hold their own, not because of their antiquity alone, which invests them with a certain glamour, but because natural variation, fine design, and individual craftsmanship will continue to win universal respect and because the resulting uniqueness adds an altogether personal quality to any ornament.

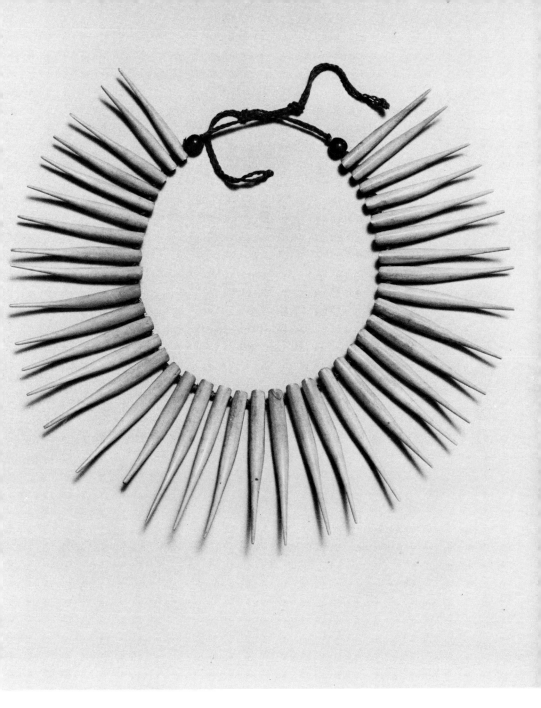

Necklace—bone, beads, sennit (Fiji Islands)

Necklace—ivory, black-and-white glass beads (Alaska; Eskimo)

Necklace—glass beads, leopard teeth (Republic of the Congo)

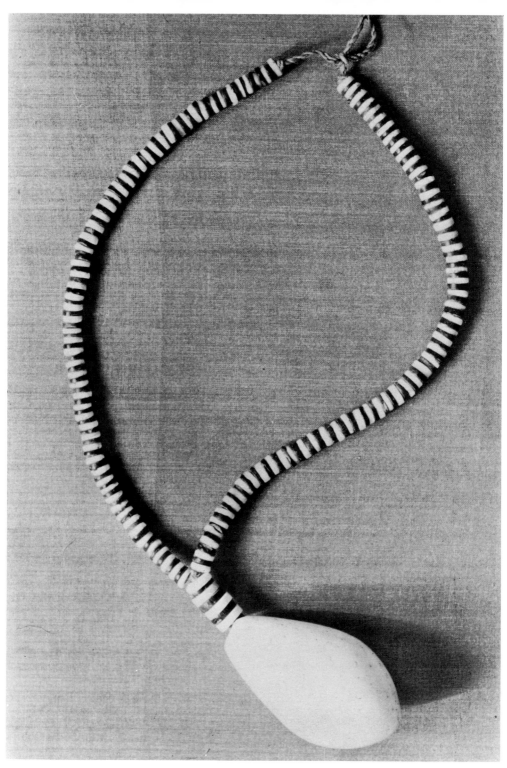

*Necklace—disks of black kokos and white conus shell with a penant of
tridacua shell (Gilbert Islands)*

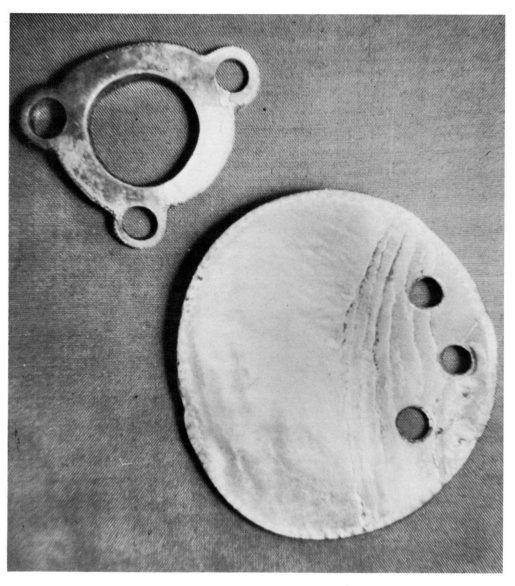

Shell Ornament (California Indians)

*Arm Band—beads of glass, banana seeds, and shell; palm leaf strips;
ornament of conus shell (New Guinea; Massim)*

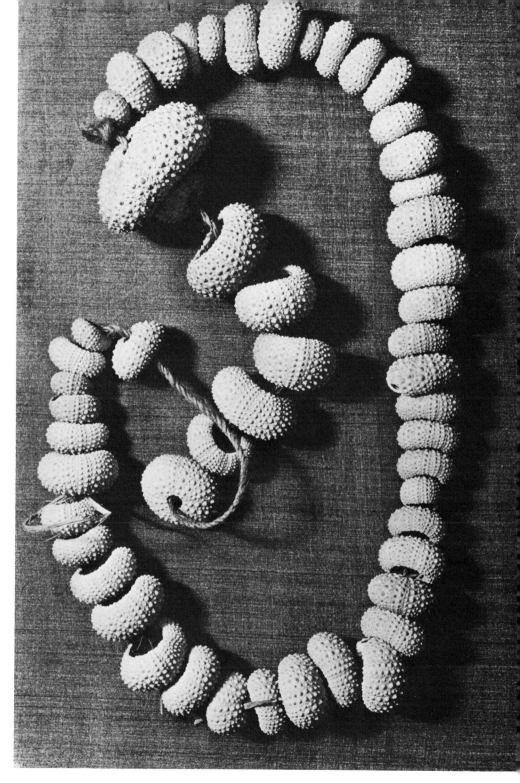

Necklace—sea urchins (Western Islands; Wuwulu)

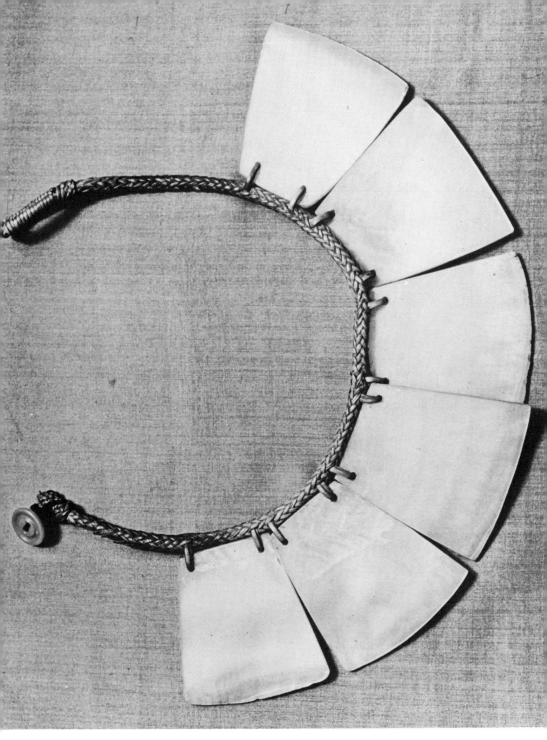

Necklace—pearl shell (Philippines)

I V

Beads and Magic

SURELY NO ONE could doubt that the power of beads is essentially a magic power. But how can one make magic explicit? Since its language is symbolic and its potency largely unconscious, it is difficult to say plainly what magic is all about. Today we protest that we do not believe in magic and yet we blow out the candles on the birthday cake, avoid the number 13, wish on the first star we see at night. Why do so many cars have a rabbit's foot or a baby's shoe hanging in the window, and why is the first lost tooth placed under a child's pillow? All of these customs can be traced to earlier, and probably more explicit, beliefs in the powers of magic acts—but they survive. The interesting point is that now, even though we "know" they are mere superstitions, we still do not quite relinquish the gestures.

Perhaps if we try to define magic we will be better able to understand both its remnants in our day and the powerful part that beads have played for people in ways of life ruled incomparably more by superstition than our own because magic complemented limited knowledge and alone promised human influence on some of the most fateful aspects of existence. For magic is and was a method of controlling those elements of life over which man has little or no power and which in the past he did not even dream of influencing by scientific means. Like the remnants of the superstitions cited, it is an attempt to influence the future: it is directed toward the avoidance of ill fortune, the protection against evil specified or unspecified, or the promotion of a powerful wish unattainable through active effort.

Anthropologists who have made extensive studies of primitive magic tell us that its practices are guided by two hypotheses. The first one is that *like produces like*, that similarity is effect as well as cause. A ruby, being red, is a powerful preventative against bleeding. Jaundice can be cured by wearing a yellow stone, for the unhealthy color of the skin and with it the sickness can be extracted by the powerful yellow of the stone. The second hypothesis is that *contact implies permanent contagion*: things that have been in contact with one another remain in some way charged and continue to act on each other. If a hunter successfully tracks and kills a bear, that animal's claws strung around his neck lend him the attributes of the bear and greatly increase his skill and his prowess.

Rationally considered, both these ideas are nonsense unless one recognizes them as a counterpart and an expression of those deepest convictions and beliefs which pervade all our interpersonal attitudes, our powerful emotions, our loves and hates, our fervent good wishes—and our evil ones. And we count on such "irrational" powers. The lift to the spirit of the sick person who is not only being taken care of but also feels cared for and *about* may be just what he needs to muster his own recuperative resources. Similarly, the proud hunter may indeed feel more vigorous and self-assured in his new regalia, the symbols of successful encounters acknowledged by his peers and elders. So magic hypotheses may work whether they are rationally or irrationally held, for in the long run we call that truth which feels right and works best—and magic is a practical art dealing with supernatural powers reinforced by human motivations.

The practical magic of beads, then, may be clarified if we consider the underlying motivations in a few specific instances. Let us take first, for example, the use of beads as protection against all the aspects of ill which we subsume under the word "harm." Harm may be specific. To fall, and especially to fall off a horse, is both inglorious and dangerous. Turquoise, so it has been believed for centuries, possesses an inherent quality which protects the individual from falling and which also makes horses, camels, and donkeys surefooted. Should one not be able to afford the luxury of turquoise, a blue bead or, better, a string of blue beads will afford the desired protection, and such strands of large turquoise-blue glazed beads may still be seen in use in parts of the Near East. No doubt firm belief in such protection and the ownership of the protecting object has helped both to make man more surefooted and more masterly in the saddle.

Donkey beads—clay with turquoise glaze

Serpentine, being usually green and marked with streaks or veins of white, is, as its name indicates, reminiscent of snakes. In some parts of Italy today, it is said, the peasants still believe that the wearing of serpentine will protect the individual from snake bites. And it is not altogether impossible that here, too, belief and possession combine to promote fearlessness which in turn calms the potential attacker. Be that as it may, the main gain is, of course, self-assurance and the assuaging of inner anxiety. In this way the innumerable specific harms to which men are exposed have been countered by an equal number of amulets specifically endowed with the corresponding necessary protective powers.

The virtue of the amulet might be inherent in its color, blue symbolizing sky and purity; red, warmth and blood; gold and amber, the quickening rays of the sun. But the magic power was also often vested in forms of abstract or representational design and in significant symbols. When craftsmen, in addition, discovered how to engrave stones a new element of protection was added to those previously available, namely the inscribed word.

The dangers for which all these varied amulets and charms were specific were ever-present and very real; a thread of deeply felt relationship, and of obvious and tangible relatedness, connected the magic power of the charm with the intended object of magic. There is a vaguely rational idea involved when a stone which incorporates the blue of the sky is believed to be endowed with power to hold its wearer up, for the blue sky is above and upholds our spirits. The color and marking of the serpentine is suggestive of a causal as well as a sympathetic relationship with the snake and this makes plausible a belief that the stone has power over it. If you endow color with all its implicit meaning, and this we still do consciously or unconsciously in our preferences and reflections, and if you associate substance and form with implicit values, then the play of the imagination in the devising of amulets, if seemingly limitless, still follows at least psychological laws, though tradition and conformity may veil the original meaning. From Egypt, preserved through centuries in the tombs of the royal dead, we have a remarkable inventory of such amulets of all shapes and forms buried with their owners to protect them even into the new life beyond.

To enable men to walk securely, with a certain control over visible dangers emanating from their immediate surroundings, then, was the province of the amulets which we have so far categorized as those promising protection against *tangible* peril.

But human beings on the whole have been more fear-ridden by the *intangible* dangers with which they feel themselves surrounded, fear of the "envy, hatred, and malice and all uncharitableness" which rests in the minds and hearts of their fellow men. Primitive peoples have almost universally attributed a fearsome power to envy and have sought to dissipate it with sanctions and magic protection. It is said that a golden-haired girl in Italy until very recently would wear a charm on her head to protect her from envious eyes. Nine of the ten commandments of the Judeo-Christian and Moslem religions deal with transgressions so tangible that one can conceive of their implementation by lawful means in an orderly society, but the tenth, "Thou shalt not covet," forbids an inner state not open to inspection and yet leading to malignancies which men fearfully respected before religions were formulated in complicated words. When we say, "I am green with envy," we must mean that envy is a sickness of the body as well as of the spirit, which we betray with unhealthy (bile green) color. It also suggests, rather uncomfortably, the poison and treachery of the snake.

But not only the malevolent thoughts of living fellow men have been feared. The very spirits of the dead may carry into their new existence the old hates and envies, and these unseen enemies are potent and omnipresent for they are anchored in our memories and in our unconscious.

Furthermore, the very moral precepts which any social group must promote in order to make a shared life possible may, as we know, only serve us to dissimulate. The injunction may be to behave courteously to one's elders, for example, or to avoid assiduously any encounter with one's mother-in-law by look, word, or deed. But, however correct behavior may be in conforming with the social taboos and regulations of the group, human feelings are betrayed by the eyes. It is the eyes which express friendliness and trust; it is also the eyes which unfeignedly reveal hatred and malice evoking a reaction of fear and discomfort in the weakest and the strongest among men.

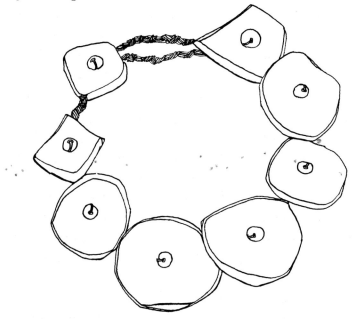

Shell disks with carnelian beads

There is a malignant power, then, in the glance of hate. It is experienced as the essence of evil itself, and men have justly named this phenomenon the "evil eye" and have devised magic means with which to protect themselves from its attack. Blue, the pure color of the sky, may shield the wearer from this danger, a single blue bead being adjudged sufficient. Do we still honor this ancient belief when we dress the bride in "something old, something new, something borrowed, and something blue"?

So amulets, carved stones, or talismans have been devised in extraordinary variety to meet man's age-old need for protection against the evil eye. But the simplest and most powerful protection is the bead itself, for it serves as the most ubiquitous symbol which has been used against the evil eye, namely the eye itself. In both Egypt and India the eye is a mystical symbol of great potency, and it has taken its place in the religious symbolism of the whole Western world. For everyday use against the evil eye a bead, called specifically the "eye bead," was early designed and produced in quantity.

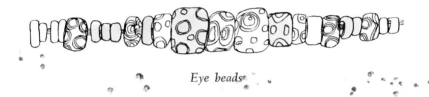

Eye beads

Gustavus A. Eisen (the archeologist who has studied these beads most extensively) has described them as follows: "Eye beads are beads of various colors, shapes and materials which are ornamented with one or more spots, often circumscribed by rings, resembling eyes. These eyes may, however, be oval, circular or triangular." On the earliest known examples of these beads the eyes are painted on the clay. Later, when glass was used, a simple drop of a darker color was pushed into the matrix of the already formed bead. Later still, techniques were devised to raise the eye from the surface of the bead with bands of different colors, thus making it protrude. The variety was enormous and the techniques employed changed as new skills were developed. The earliest clay "eye beads" which can be dated are Egyptian from the Nineteenth Dynasty, but the manufacture of these beads continued for hundreds of years.

Eye beads traveled all over the world. Where they have been manufactured in areas distant from Egypt, such as China, they have taken on some of the characteristic features of their wearers' eyes—for how else could they serve their purpose of distracting and averting the evil glance of other people? The Chinese eye beads, therefore, do not have the eye in the center of the circle or group of concentric circles. The form is stylized and definitely Oriental in effect.

Chinese eye beads

In Brittany today the peasants still cherish among their most valued possessions strings of beads which include eye beads of ancient manufacture. These beads are believed to exercise such great protective and curative power that their owners are unwilling to part with them at any price, and necklaces of these beads are inherited from one generation to the next and carefully guarded as bonded security against life's ills. In Africa, too, eye beads add a patterned and colorful note to the native necklaces. A whole necklace of eye beads, however, all "looking" in different directions, is a truly disquieting sight. The viewers eyes are first drawn to look at it but soon feel disturbed rather than charmed and shift away with

Modern eye bead

relief, proving the ornament to be an effective and cleverly devised defensive charm.

However, protection is not enough. Man also needs additional powers of attack. He has always had good reason to feel himself less well endowed than the animals around him from an aesthetic point of view, and also to envy them as stronger, swifter, more courageous, and endowed with keener senses. Hunters almost invariably seem to have a profound respect for the animals who are their prey. They admire them for the very attributes which they themselves lack. There were two possible ways to deal with this situation. Man could invent tools and weapons to extend his physical capacities, and he could devise charms to increase his own courage, to sharpen his senses and his wit, and to provide himself with added power and confidence. For this the hunter had to identify himself with his prey. Primitive tribes and clans have animal names and religiously perform animal dances, propitiating the spirits of the animals that they most revere. And hunters wear the skins of their prey and decorate themselves with the claws, the teeth or tusks, and the bones. Such decoration is admired for its ornamental effect but, as pointed out, there is much more to it than mere decoration. The wearing of a tiger's teeth directly imbues the wearer with the fierce strength of the tiger, the ivory charm bestows the tremendous power of the elephant, the porcupine quill makes the aimed arrow more deadly. And, as indicated, the universality of the use of the natural biting, piercing, scratching tools of animals for the magic decoration of primitive men suggests that in some measure they did promote courageous action and inspire confidence. But there were also humans who seemed to belong to a different species, and in order to incorporate the strength of human enemies it was magically desirable to acquire and preserve some parts of human victims. The teeth or knuckle bones of the erstwhile enemy worn around the neck or arm added new vitality to the victorious warrior.

But beyond man and beast there were still nature's fickle elements, which provided problems of a vastly different order. Unpredictability has always been one of their main characteristics. A sudden storm on sea or land has always been traumatically destructive; heavy winds, freezing temperatures, and drought could bring sudden disruption and disaster—flood and earthquake leave man helpless and terrified. Against such elemental dangers, too, protective charms were worn to guard the individual.

Sailors and travelers have been among the most eager customers for amulets and talismans as protection from wind and sea, from cold, and from blistering heat. In a fragment of the manuscript of a Greek lapidary, probably written between 200 and 300 A.D. and quoted by G. F. Kunz in *Curious Lore of Precious Stones*, we find a list of amulets, seven in number, to be worn by sailors. The first is composed of a carbuncle and a chalcedony, which were protection against drowning. The second was made up of a stone likened to ice—probably rock-crystal—and an Indian stone, "clear but silvery," possibly corundum. The third, a beryl, "transparent, brilliant, and of a sea-green hue," protected the wearer against fear. The "druops white in the center," which was probably the variety of agate resembling an eye and thus considered to be a potent protection against the evil eye, was the fourth charm. As a fifth, coral is listed, which was to be strung with strips of seal skin to the prow of the ship, guarding it from heavy winds and waves. A striped stone, perhaps a banded agate, to be worn to protect the wearer from the surging of the sea is number six. The last mentioned is "opsianos," possibly a kind of jet which was generally protective for all who traveled by water.

Perhaps the most telling evidence of a search for control of the powers of the universe by means of magic is the extensive work of ancient scholars on the astral qualities of stones. By some calculation, now difficult for us to follow, certain stones were ascribed to the planets:

SAPPHIRE—SATURN   EMERALD—VENUS

JACINTH—JUPITER   AGATE—MERCURY

DIAMOND—SUN   SELENITE—MOON

RUBY—MARS

This list, we are told by G. F. Kunz, is Chaldaean, but the planets were thought to be related to more than one stone so that each gem was in some way attributed to a heavenly body. The color and appearance of the stone were not merely symbolic of the nature of the planet but were supposed to exercise a sympathetic quality, to attract the planet's beneficient influence and provide a medium for the transmission of this virture to the wearer. And if a stone were in addition engraved with the sign of the planet and the zodiacal symbols appropriate to the wearer's birth date, it was the more efficacious in bringing his life into harmony with the heavenly bodies presiding over his horoscope.

The ancient writers insist that the image graven on the stone was in itself of no virtue. The talisman became imbued with vital quality by the influence of the stars during whose ascendancy the work had been executed. It was mandatory that the engraving be done while the planet was in the asscendant and the design engraved emblematic of it. During the process of engraving, reflections from a mirror which had been exposed to the planet's rays were cast upon the stone. This complicated procedure facilitated the merging of the influence of the planet with the essence of the stone and assured the potency of its talismanic virtue to the wearer. The harder stones were capable of retaining the celestial virtues longer than softer materials. But every stone possessed stored-up energy derived from the stars and planets and was therefore peculiarly sensitive to the emanations of certain stars or groups of stars. Thus, the possibilities of individualizing talismans for those who could afford to have them made was unending. Such charms were considered so personal

Carved stone beads

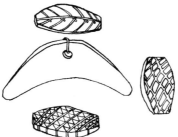

that when worn they became a part of the very body and soul of the wearer, and were therefore to be carefully guarded. This deeply felt desire for harmony with astral influence, then, gave rise to a highly complicated pseudo-science, a subject for specialists which occupied the minds of erudite scholars and the hands of skilled craftsmen.

We have, so far, concentrated on the power of the individual bead rather than on the complex aspect of form in the designing of necklaces which would tie the story of beads more closely to the more comprehensive topic of jewelry. Let this be illustrated by only one strikingly simple example of the convergence of design, nature, and magic meaning. The previously mentioned excavations at Ur have apparently demonstrated beyond question the historical fact of the great deluge, the subject of the most famous Babylonian legend—the biblical version of which is the story of Noah's flood. As a token of His promise that such a flood would never again occur, God sent Noah and his people the rainbow—that arc of radiant color the natural causes of which we now "understand," but which we still greet with awe and wonder. The Babylonian legend of the great flood, however, though similar in most other details, ends with the placing of a necklace of lapis lazuli around the neck of their goddess Isthar. The similarity in form of these two symbols of divine promise cannot fail to strike us: indeed there is something of a rainbow in a necklace and of a necklace in a rainbow. This is eminently exemplified by both the Assyrian necklace of many strands and the Egyptian broad collar.

The rainbow leads us back from heaven to earth. Whatever symbolic relationship we may conjecture from the two versions of the flood legend, wider-ranging associations lead us to the fact that the Chinese symbol of a half "pi" represents a rainbow—and a fertility symbol. And, indeed, we have not touched yet on another vital area of human life where magic has been evoked to influence the unpredictable. For beyond the province of human control also lies the whole area of the fertility of women, as well as the virility

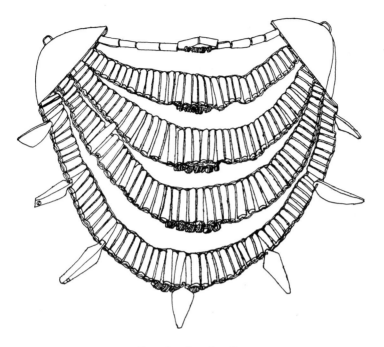

Egyptian broad collar

of men and the productivity of the earth and its relation to the gift of water. Here again magic was called upon to play its part. In ancient China, the *huang* was portrayed by an arc, sometimes in the form of a dragon or a fish. The fish seems to have been in general a symbol of fertility (and, incidentally, of watchfulness: they have no eyelids and remain, therefore, ever alert). Fish, through a process of metamorphosis, become dragons at the spring equinox, and the dragon is regarded as the "genius of the seas, rivers, lakes, mists and the principal of water generally"—a fertility symbol, then, directly related to the rain deity.

FROM THE merely protective properties of stones we have progressed to the consideration of their positive power to influence human,

natural, and even astral forces. However, there is more to report on
the extensive belief in their curative properties, to which ancient
medicine devoted much study. The rationale for ascribing medicinal properties to stones was, of course, also based on the pervasive
acceptance of all forms of sympathetic magic. The young Brahman
boy was told, "Tread on this stone: like a stone be firm," exempli-
fying once more the manner in which virtues attributed to stones
could be assimilated by a process of contagion. But, we must now
add, the stone itself must be "healthy."

In the Sacred Books of Hindus it is stated, "The gem that has
its appropriate color and lustre and *is devoid of any defects* is
beneficial to beauty, growth, fame, valor and life. Others are known
to be injurious." Specific virtues are ascribed to particular stones
but the general belief in India was that the real power of the stone
lay in its perfection.

Early evidence of the use of specific stones for circumscribed
medicinal purposes is found in the Ebers Papyrus from Egypt. Here
are statements recommending lapis lazuli as an ingredient for eye
salve and hematite, an iron oxide for checking hemorrhages and for
reducing inflammations. Whether there was in these prescriptions
any "rational" consideration of the chemical constituents of the
stones we cannot know. However, an eye salve made of "kalil" in
India was administered with the following spell: "The sharpness
of the stone art thou, protect my eye."

Much of what we know of ancient belief in the therapeutic
properties of stones we learn from Pliny's Natural History. Although he himself seems to have accepted the information he
gathered with considerable skepticism, he nevertheless recorded and
preserved for us the inherited and still prevalent beliefs of the first
century A.D., which remained in popular acceptance for hundreds of
years. We learn, for example, that the red stones—ruby, spinel,
garnet, carnelian, and bloodstone—have an affinity with blood and
are therefore efficacious in controlling hemorrhages. Since rarity

and value increased the remedial qualities of stones, the ruby was prized most highly for this purpose. The yellow stones were remedies for bilious disorders and jaundice. Plutarch gives another interesting example of this general belief in the healing power of the color yellow. The stone curlew was kept by medical practitioners to be used as an antidote for jaundice, but the virtue of the bird lay exclusively in the color of its large golden eye, which was capable of drawing the yellow skin color out of the patient. Plutarch adds the practical note that the bird is usually kept covered in its cage to prevent the occurence of gratis cures.

Green stones, we learn, are curative for many diseases but especially for weakness of the eyes. This very early documented belief (Theophrastus, third century B.C.) is affirmed today in the generality that nature has provided so much green to which the human eye is adjusted that this "natural" color rests and restores. It is also interesting to read that the craftsmen of ancient times whose work was most demanding on the eyes, the engravers, kept a green stone, preferably an emerald, on their workbenches so that they could occasionally rest their eyes upon it and thus refresh themselves.

The amethyst, quite understandably, was believed to have a close relationship with the grape and thus to wine. It was the gem of sobriety but had the added property of keeping the wearer immune to the effects of overindulgence in intoxicating drink. Should the gem itself not prove powerful enough to steady the drinker it was suggested that a cup formed of this stone when filled with water would appear to be filled with rich wine and the drinker, playing appearance against essence, could remain astonishingly unaffected by unlimited drinking.

In the areas of the world where turquoise is highly prized it is endowed with universal remedial powers against all the ills of body and mind. In Persia it has been credited with great potency as a sovereign remedy for diseases of the eye, hernia, dyspepsia, insanity, and ulcers, and also as a dependable antidote for snake and scorpion bites.

Jade, too, in China and early Mexico, was endowed with great therapeutic power. The English word itself is derived from the Spanish *piedra de jade*, which means stone of the loins. It was first known in English as nephrite or the "kidney stone" in recognition of the legendary medicinal properties with which it was endowed.

Whatever the stone, however, its curative powers were thought to be enhanced by engraving. A combination of the symbol and the word were held in high regard, and an engraved stone thus became a very potent charm capable of fending off illness and, if prevention failed, of curing with dispatch. As to specific procedures, the usual method was to touch the patient with the stones or to prescribe their being worn next to the afflicted body area. Close proximity was important, and we read with some relief that the emerald after having been applied to diseased eyes should be washed in cold water in order to insure its continued effectiveness.

In about 130 A.D., Galen wrote the following account of how the stone was applied and his personal report concerning the apparently disputed effectiveness of engraved symbols: "Some have testified to a virtue in certain stones, and this is true of the green jasper, that is to say, this stone aids the stomach and navel by contact. And some, therefore, set the stone in rings and engrave on it a dragon surrounded by rays, according to what King Necheopsos has transmitted to posterity in the fourteenth book [of his works]. Indeed, I myself have thoroughly tested this stone, for I hung a necklace composed of them about my neck so that they touched the navel, and I received not less benefit from them than I would had they borne the engraving of which Necheopsos wrote."* Who could deny the evidence of such a rigorously scientific experiment?

* G. F. Kunz, *Curious Lore of Precious Stones*

Stones were also ground into fine powder and drunk in wine or honey. Here we run into what must have presented great economic problems, for who but the very wealthy could afford to grind up emeralds and rubies as medicine? Sometimes, perhaps when the diagnosis of an illness was particularly difficult, the recommended curative dose was composed of a variety of precious stones. Arnobio, in his *Tesoro delle Gioie*, gives a recipe for "the most noble electuary of jacinth." Included in this formula was jacinth, emerald, sapphire, topaz, garnet, pearl, ruby, white and red coral, and amber. If none of these ingredients effected a cure, at least the attending physician could not be accused of neglect. Pope Clement VII became seriously ill in 1534. He was attended, so we are told, by physicians who prescribed medicine made up of various precious stones, including diamonds. A single dose of these costly powders was valued at three thousand ducats and the fourteen-day treatment which resulted, not too surprisingly, in the pope's demise is said to have cost forty thousand ducats.

If engraving could enhance the healing power of a stone then it follows that sculpturing it into appropriate forms could only increase its power by adding strong pointers toward specific uses.

Amulets of stone or glazed clay which represent parts of the body are numerous in present collections of ancient beads. These are rather naturalistic in form and were often executed with great attention to detail. The magic thought implicit in such careful execution seems to have been that the perfect representation of the leg, for example, worn next to the body will strengthen the corresponding member of the wearer and at the same time serve to extract from it by a sympathetic process the ill from which it may be suffering. Hands, too, and feet, arms, penises, breasts, and heads, as well as eyes, noses, and ears, can all be clearly identified, and it seems fairly conclusive that their function was to benefit the corresponding body part of the wearer.

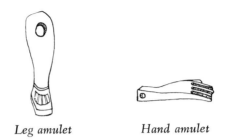

Leg amulet   *Hand amulet*

From such specific therapeutic details we now turn to more general concerns, for men have sought not only defined goals and protection against concrete afflictions in their great variety but also the less well-defined blessings in the form of wealth, honor, happiness, and longevity. These elements of the abundant life, too, were among the benefits which stones might bestow upon their owners. Consider the power of the bloodstone amulet as described in the Leyden Papyrus:

"The world has no greater thing; if any one have this with him he will be given whatever he asks for; it also assuages the wrath of kings and despots, and whatever the wearer says will be believed. Whoever bears this stone, which is a gem, and pronounces the name engraved upon it, will find all doors open, while bonds and stone walls will be rent asunder."

The turquoise, too, being both generous and powerful, bestows immeasurable wealth on the person who gazes first on the new moon and then on this stone. That prosperity should be one of the gifts of fate secured by precious jewels is somewhat ironical considering the fact that to own them one must have already reached this happy estate. Honor or at least status follows prosperity to some degree. Happiness, however, must be blessed with the help of more concrete magic. Amulets such as the Chinese carved stones representing a pair of geese or the double fish image, both symbolizing wedded bliss, are worn to insure such felicity.

Pearls are endowed with magic power to bring fulfillment to the lover. Longevity might be conferred on the wise, according to Taoist philosophers, when they regularly drank a "divine liquor" made of jade ground into a powder, boiled in a copper pot, and mixed with equal parts of rice and dew water. Jade swallowed under particularly fortunate conditions could, in any case, enable a man to live for a thousand years.

If stones had such sweeping powers, it is not surprising that their essence was also thought to be related to the supreme ideals of man. "Truth" is represented by the color blue and ascribed to lapis lazuli by the Egyptians, and to the sapphire, the stone of purity, by others. But wherever man senses the ideal he will attempt to use such powers for evil as well as for sacred purposes. The sapphire, endowed with the power to influence spirits, was therefore extolled both as the ecclesiastical stone and as an indispensable tool of black magic. Bartolomaeus Anglicus wrote, in 1495, "Also wytches love well this stone, for they wene that they may werke certen wondres by vertue of this stone." Thus white magic and black magic have kept step with one another through the ages, as has the medicine man with the witch. The same stone which exerts the most positive good may, under evil influences, be enlisted in the cause of black and sinister bedevilment.

And finally, approaching the borderline between sculptured beads and miniature sculpture, carved stones represented the gods themselves. Their images are included in burials in those areas of the world where the gods have been given human form. In Egypt and Assyria, in Greece and Italy the gods are also often represented in the form of their animal counterparts, the guise in which they sometimes appeared on earth. Such belief in the ability of the gods to assume animal form brings them within the range of familiarity of the man closely bound to nature, and serves both to deify the chosen animal and to make the attributes of the god more earthly and knowable. The goat and the lamb, the turtle and the frog, the hippopotamus, the lion and the hawk, the ibis and the eagle have all served as the earthly incarnations of gods. Their images were carved in stones, formed out of clay and glass, and cast in gold. Worn on the person, the proximity of the deities was assured. As one would not forget their presence, so would one not be forgotten.

Egyptian amulets

In their loving concern for the dead, and as an expression of hope in a life after death, men have placed such carved and engraved images on the bodies of those to be buried. The favored form in Egypt was the scarab. It represented the principle of life— the pulse of time, the heart. Engraved with the thirtieth chapter of the Book of the Dead, it was worn over the heart of the mummy as a symbol of the heart of Isis.

Beetle   *Scarab*

An important amulet frequently mentioned in ancient Chinese texts was a stone in the form of a cicada which was placed on the tongue of the dead. The cicada was the symbol of resurrection because of its natural history, for only after a long period of underground existence as larva did the adult insect split its confining skin and emerge. The souls of the dead, too, so the Chinese believed, would emerge to new life from their graves.

The Aztecs, however, endowed unsculptured stones themselves with life-giving power. In fact, they expressed the conviction that at one time all men were stones, and they included in the burials of their dead a small green stone which they called the principle of life. This concept faces us with the paradox that what is usually considered the coldest and most inanimate substance, stone, can come to represent the very origin and the warmth of life. Yet, that stones are endowed with a kind of life of their own is an ancient belief. Indeed, amber, as has already been noted, could be charged with magnetic force and was also found .from time to time in a strange form—imprisoning small creatures. There were other stones which were magnetic and this attribute gave them an energetic kind of existence. Stones strangely sculptured by nature—representing a human form or a body part or, perhaps, ancient symbols—were suggestive of previous life. Fossilized sea forms or stones with strange markings were thought to be of miraculous origin since there was no knowledge of ossification. And stones could seem alive in other strange ways. Some, like turquoise, were known to change color while being worn, sky blue turning slowly pale and green, a consequence, in fact, of proximity to the warmth of the body. The turquoise was then thought to have fallen ill, perhaps in sympathy with its owner! Pearls likewise sometimes lose their luster, and coral may fade, surely suggesting the loss of vital quality in the once healthy stone. And if precious gems varied from day to day in the depth of their color and brilliance, these changes could only be understood as presaging events in the lives of those who wore them. In fact, some stones were said to have cracked when misadventure came the way of their owners.

Finally, the search for a means of creating precious stones and gold became in itself a matter of earnest concern. They came, after all, from the bowels of the earth. Luminous gems and brilliant gold were found in a matrix of ugly, otherwise unremarkable stone or dirt. Were they the product of dirt? Alchemists were untiring in their efforts to rival the feat of nature and to reproduce earth's most precious materials out of common clay. Again we are aware of a mysterious polarity, that of Dirt and Purity, of worthless matter and gem or gold, which is reminiscent of those all-inclusive polarities of Divine and Evil, of Life and Death.

Yin Yang symbol

Today in displays of the world's most famous jewels, public attention is directed to two facts. The informative signs state how many carats each stone weighs and suggest its exchange value. In the face of such overweaning commercial appraisal one is reluctant to press more impractical reflections. And yet—how many centuries did it take for this stone to be formed under the earth, what are the legends relative to its magic power, was it worn with pride and delight, or was the evil eye of envy upon it with resulting tragic consequences? Money may be our modern magic, and the wonderful and the miraculous may belong to another era. But the exclusive emphasis on weight and cost surely do an injustice not only to the beauty of the stones but also to those men who have preserved them through the years possibly because they cherished them for more profound and personal reasons than their mere resale value. Deep and ancient emotions remain which will, if ever so secretly, continue to be stirred by lovely stones for their color and light, for their special uniqueness and timelessness—their innate touch of magic.

Drinking Hara—horn, beads (Cameroun)

Bead Work (Egypt; Twenty-fifth Dynasty)

Doll—wood, seeds, glass beads, cowrie shells, fiber (Cameroun)

Shrunken Head—feather and beetle-back ornamentation (*Jivaro, Ecuador*)

*Boy's Initiation Mask—wood, cowrie shells, red kisi seeds
(Mali; Bambara)*

Ornament—shells, fiber, paint, cane (Papua, New Guinea)

Ibeji Figure—wood, cloth, cowrie shells, beads (Nigeria; Yoruba)

Evil-Eye Charm—shell money, glass beads (New Ireland)

V

On the Meaning of Beads

NOT LONG AGO I watched a little girl stringing beads. Her head was bent with complete absorption over a box containing a many-colored selection. Her hands were skillful and just the right size to handle the small globes of glass. In one hand she held a thread, with the other she spread out the assortment, selecting one bead or another to hold up singly to the light. Then, having made her choice, she licked the end of the thread and slipped it through the bead. After a number of beads were successfully strung the whole string was held up for appraisal. As she held it with both hands and moved it so that the light danced in the colored forms, a slow smile expressed her satisfaction before she bent her head once more and proceeded with her painstaking work.

For thousands of years this same engrossing activity has employed the fingers and the concentrated attention of young and old people all over the world and for them as for the busy child this truly playful and yet quite serious undertaking could challenge genuinely creative effort.

How can one understand this primary attraction of beads? What is their fundamental appeal? We have been gathering and sorting evidence from the past in regard to the many meanings beads have had, the many roles they have played. The complex evidence is more baffling than helpful in answering the simple question of their immediate fascination, which must be the basis of their importance. Have they meant so many things and were they endowed with all these meanings in order to justify a more primitive and therefore more obscure fascination? For the only obvious connection between the absorbed child's observable behavior and all the facts, events, and meanings with which we have dealt can be reduced to the words "beauty" and "joy," which are combined in the meaning of our word "jewelry." But then we are again faced with the original query as to why light playing on rounded shapes gives delight. There must be something elemental about this human reaction, something akin to instinctive. Indeed, there are animals, like the bower bird, that seek out and display glittering things in order to lure mates to their nests, a fact which suggests a basis in biological evolution for our analogous pleasure in bright objects. Yet, man's aesthetic preoccupation with the aligning and arranging of selected objects of beauty both includes and seems to go far beyond our subject matter, the bead. So far, we have emphasized that beads have come to mean many things to many people and that their "meaning" is often carried by the momentum of mere tradition and habituation. Yet, if anything as "trifling" as a bead has retained such ubiquity throughout the history of the species, there must be hidden in it also some meaning essential in the life of each single individual.

One important lead, I feel strongly (and feel as a mother as

well as a craftsman, if such a "primitive" judgment may enter a discourse of this kind), is offered by the science of human development which has taught us to look for the nature of some of our most elemental feelings and responses in the earliest years, in first reactions to life. Babies new to this world react to a variety of stimuli both from within and without, but their first smile, we have learned from exact observation, is in response to a mother's, or at any rate a human, face. And a smile is an exclusively human reaction. Such confirmation of mutuality, then, such a first clear affirmation with an unequivocal facial expression of pleasure in a basic relationship may perhaps not be evoked by the mother without quite a performance on her part of smiling, nodding, and making a variety of coaxing sounds. Yet the baby's responding smile is experienced as a triumph and is of course claimed by her as a token of her child's recognition of her presence and personality. Science, in its sober way, however—and not, we hope, to the detriment of future mother-child relationships—has shown exactly what it does take to evoke a baby's smile. Psychologists have discovered that any smiling face hovering over the baby brings forth a responding smile, that even a light round mask does the same trick, and, finally, that all that is *really* required is a bright, more or less spherical surface with two dark round spots painted on it or two beads attached to it in a horizontal configuration resembling eyes.*
The baby, then, is born ready to react at an early age to the eyes— the eyes which have been described since time immemorial as shining, laughing, dancing, glowing, glaring, gleaming—like beads— and which are, like beads, colored blue, green, gray, brown, golden. They are truly, as Anglo-Saxon literature has it, the head jewels. It is with the eyes, then, that mother and child communicate be-

---

* Peter H. Wolff, "Observations on the Early Development of Smiling," Proceedings, Tavistock Study Group on Mother-Infant Interaction, London (1959); and René A. Spitz, "The Smiling Response: A Contribution to the Ontogenesis of Social Relations," Genetic Psychology Monographs, Vol. 34 (August 1964), Clark University.

fore speech develops, and the meeting of eyes will serve as an adjunct to speech and whenever language fails. It is with the eyes that concern and love are communicated, and distance and anger as well. Could it be for this genetic reason, then, that the attraction of round, shining, colorful objects has taken on such powerful meaning for man, the "alienated" creature? What could support such an assumption?

When a baby is being nursed his eyes will seek the mother's. On occasion, if she turns her face away, he will cry. When several adults surround a baby his gaze will move, not from face to face, but from one pair of eyes to another. A pair of earrings or other bright objects may temporarily become the focus of his attention, but essentially it is the eyes with which he seems to feel himself surrounded, which he studies and with which he communicates. To him the face is at first only vaguely modeled, mouths make many movements, but the eyes shine out with a lively reflected light.

The eyes, then, I would submit, may well be a basic clue to the elemental power of rounded shining objects. We begin life with this relatedness to eyes, and when our eyes are able to perceive both detail and distance we still communicate with our fellow men, faster than with words and in many ways more truly, by means of our eyes. We are warmed by the friendly eye, the eye of love; chilled by the hate and envy expressed in the evil eye; frustrated by the blank look of no communication which makes us long to see the eyes of one whom we fear may have grown distant or turned away from us.

Have the beads which man has worn for all the practical and aesthetic reasons already enumerated also served as his magically endowed "extra eyes" underscoring all other meanings? We cannot here dwell on the many functions which the eyes and the face play in the evolution of man, this upright animal who "faces" his kind and his world. His beads, at any rate, could see backward and sideward as well as forward, and their protection around the vulnerable throat may well have taken over the function of the ruff of his animal forebears. If so, this would, of course, be only one aspect of a many-sided development which at some unknown point in prehistory made man stand up, thus to be both more naked and more exposed than other animals—but freeing his hands to work, to make the things dictated by his extraordinary brain guided by his extraordinary vision. He invented tools to work with and weapons to increase his prowess as hunter, and this gave him food and clothing. But beyond the protection of his body he craved feathers, claws, teeth, quills with which to ornament himself, for being looked at as well as looking have great significance not only for his biological survival but also for his social status. He used all these objects, too, as magic, in ceremonies, and as dance paraphernalia in order to acquire through them some of the admired and feared attributes of animals—their skill, strength, and cunning. And especially he gained through this ornamentation of his body a sense of relatedness to his tribe, a visible display of his rank within his group as well as a stronger sense of his own distinct identity as expressed in the things worn on his person. For man, being less powerful physically than the animals around him, developed into a cultural animal, finding strength and protection in gregariousness, cooperative venture, and social stratification.

Being erect, a tool man, our ancestor with the extraordinary brain also developed an acute curiosity, and since he could see very far he began to observe the heavens, the sun, the moon, and the stars. Less a creature of instinct than other animals, he tried to understand the universe in which he found himself. If he used his mind to invent tools and to organize into social groups, he also declared himself human by seeking answers to mystical questions and by finding his first vague reassurances in the nebulous area of magic.

Man everywhere has reverently propitiated the sun, the moon, and the stars. Awesome in their remoteness and divinely pursuing their slow progress through the spacious skies with regularity and unhuman unconcern, they were his day and his night, his months and his years. He sought to win their benevolent attention by all the magical means he could devise. He made round forms, disks and spheres—forms which have universally been the objects, the symbols, of greatest veneration. The heavenly eyes, I submit, then, are the second major source of inspiration for man's use of beads as jewelry.

Among their earliest finds of amber in northern Europe and Russia are disks with a hole in the center, described earlier, and this form is one of the most prevalent among the ancient burial treasures of Central America, formed there out of jade. The gold disks "like small mirrors which they wore about their necks" were the ornaments of the Indians of the new world discovered by Columbus. Our Indians of the Southwest, too, still wear such disks made of bone, inlaid with bits of turquoise. The Chinese *yin yang* circle, which makes visual the belief in the interrelatedness and interdependence of beginning and end, is another elaboration of this form, and the list could be augmented with the description of other examples from all over the world. In general, the significance

Ancient perforated disk

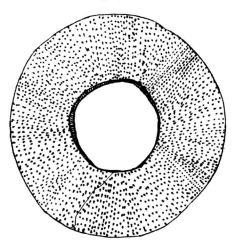

of the disk is that it represents wholeness, completedness; it is the essence of perfection. Small spheres, then, are magic microcosms mirroring the remote light-giving forms of the macrocosm of the universe.

Now man has invented artificial light, light that is more garish, more dazzling than the stars and the moon, and with it he turns night into day. He has made satellites and he has harnessed the terrible power of the sun. We now take the light for granted, and we have learned to endanger our own species with the man-controlled power of the atom. The history of the simple bead, however, which has in these pages reminded us of so much in man that is cruel, vain, and avaricious, also reaffirms some universal truths.

Light was once a gift for which man was reverently grateful. It partook of that which was miraculous, like life itself. He delighted in all its forms and in the symbols which he devised to represent it. Not being able to conceive of not being, he buried his dead with concern for their next life. Into the grave he placed food, flints to make light, and the beads which had been, as it were, a part of the individuation of the loved person on this earth. Lucky the man who takes leave of the world with these thoughtful gifts offered with such human care.

If the eye is, indeed, that *ur*-form which we apprehend and take in visually with our mother's milk, we should expect to find its impress in our deepest feelings and longings and thus also in those universal manifestations of these emotions—in the symbols and forms of religion. Before gods had names now known to us, before the age of written communication, a deity existed whose worship can be traced from the earliest archeological findings in Asia to northern Europe. This deity, however crudely depicted as statue or graven image, has three characteristic attributes: eyes, a necklace of beads, and breasts. The staring eyes, however, are the dominant feature from which her modern name, the Eye Goddess, is derived.

Her temple in Tel Brak, in the Khabur Valley in eastern Syria, has now been named the Eye Temple and dated at about 3000 B.C. The eye idols excavated there share a "rigid frontality—the same staring eyes heavily outlined with colour; even the same pattern of dots to indicate strings of beads," the eyes being "the feature of the divinity which struck the beholder most forcibly." This image with its necklace and staring eyes, considered to be indisputably connected with fertility cults, can be traced as far north as Ireland and Britain, south to Central Africa, and west to the Indus Valley where the Harappa figurines also have clearly defined blobs for eyes and for their necklace beads.*

Eye Goddess of Syria

If primitive magic and infantile experience can be related to one another—and much speaks for this assumption—then this ancient deity might be described as the infant's-eye view mother goddess, for her attributes are those within the infant's cognitive universe. The breasts and the nipples (the rosette is also her symbol) provide him with warm, soothing, thirst-quenching nourishment. Her eyes commune with him, they are his community. And the beads of the necklace, so we have postulated, provide a shiny multi-

* Osbert G. S. Crawford, *The Eye Goddess*

ple stimulus which may sustain him when the mothering eye is temporarily diverted.

Modern Syrian rosette

The heir to this ancient Eye Goddess in the Egyptian hierarchy of gods was Horus, son of Osiris. In his mythological struggle with Set, the god of storm, he lost one eye, his left eye, which was later restored. Horus is the god of the heavens and reportedly his eyes symbolize the sun and the moon. The moon waxes, wanes, and disappears and is then slowly restored, even as the fruits of the

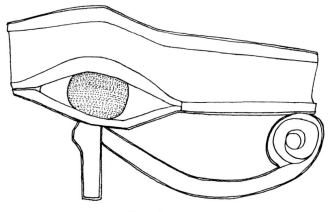

Eye of Horus

earth, even as man himself. The left eye of Horus (the feminine eye) as a symbol, then, represents the cycle of birth, death, and rebirth. But the conflict between Set and Horus was to avenge Osiris and, therefore, the lost eye was a sacrifice to Osiris. The phrase "I give to thee the eye of Horus" throughout Egyptian writings signifies the presentation of a sacrifice. In ancient Egypt the eye of Horus and the scarab (also an eye form) were the two most common symbols. "The eye of Horus acquired such a reputation that to it were ascribed peculiar strength, vigour, protective power, and safety, the rays of whose light nourished the spirits of heaven, and created things and beings."*

To the east in the villages of India a mother goddess was and still is worshiped, especially by the lower castes. There is considerable evidence that this mother goddess reigned supreme all over the Indian continent before the advent of the Aryans from the north with their male deities. The mother goddess, the Mata, is an all-seeing deity embracing birth and death—creation and destruction, the energy of the universe. The supreme god figure of the Brahmanical gods is Siva with his consort Parvati and the masculine and feminine virtues are appropriately divided between them. However, Siva is endowed with a third eye, an eye in the middle of his forehead which usually remains closed. When opened under extreme provocation it flashes out death-dealing rays of destruction.

Better known to us in the Western world are the references in the books of the Bible, to the eye of God, the great Jehovah. No graven image might be made in His likeness by the Hebrews, but their sacred writings abound with poetic expressions descriptive of His all-seeing eye. Perhaps there is some relationship between this heritage of poetic writing and the injunction against the fashioning of holy images, and for this we can be grateful since the word pictures have endured undamaged through time. If the graphic artist is endowed with "bountiful eyes," "seeing eyes," and records the form of his vision in color, light, movement, and expression, the bard, the seer, and the poet have been artists of the word often depicted as blind, lonely, and infirm. The gift of prophecy, it is said, may be bought only at the price of the right eye, for one eye of him who

* Samuel A. Mercer, *Horus, Royal God of Egypt*

sees the past and the future must be turned inward in reflection.

Herbert Read speaks of the eye of infancy and of childhood as the "innocent eye" in his book of that title. This is surely the eye that perceives out of the pure pleasure of exercising its natural function with, as he says, "virgin sensibility." Some of this quality may be preserved in maturity and is essential in the artist; but how is it lost? What is the guilty eye? The poet who composed the third chapter of Genesis, in describing the temptation and fall of Adam and Eve, puts the following words into the mouth of the "subtil" snake as he tempts with the forbidden fruit: "For God doth know that in the day ye eat thereof, then *your eyes shall be opened*, and ye shall be as gods, knowing good and evil. And when Eve *saw* that the tree was good for food, and that it was *pleasant to the eyes*, and a tree to be desired to make one wise she did eat the fruit and shared it with Adam. And the *eyes of both were opened*, and they knew that they were naked." And they covered themselves with fig leaves and hid for shame.

So, it would seem, the price of wisdom, of the knowledge of good and evil, is the loss of the innocent eye. Looking is no longer enough in itself. Looking becomes a means to an end, a tool—we lose paradise,. and are left with a deep and abiding nostalgia. But the prophets exhort the Edenless descendants of Adam and Eve and hold out hope and comfort, for "he whose eye is open" and obeys the law will see that "the commandment of the Lord is pure, enlightening the eyes." For those that turn away from His holy ways there is threat. "When ye spread forth your hands I will hide mine eyes from you," but for those that lead a godly life there is promise, "For I will set mine eyes upon them for good."

The Bible abounds in imagery concerning the eye of God which is upon His people and "runs to and fro throughout the whole earth" giving light and gracious blessing. In the Byzantine Christian churches, perhaps as a heritage from Asia Minor, the eye of God is again depicted in graphic form looking down from wall or

The circle, being without beginning or end, is a sign of
God or of Eternity. It is a symbol of the sleeping eye of God;
"The Spirit of God moved upon the face of the waters."
The open eye of God, the purpose of Revelation;
"And God said, Let there be light."*

ceiling and with pervading glance encompassing and penetrating the innermost thoughts and feelings of the assembled congregation. Among the manifestations of Western religious symbolism, too, we should not overlook the ring, the crown, and the halo.

The bead has led us to the disk and the sphere, symbols which "encompass the whole in an instant." The symbol has led us to its possible archetype, its *ur*-form, the eye.

Might one not then speculate that the eye, the eye itself as an object, is the *ur*-phenomenon of aesthetic visual delight? In *The Innocent Eye*, Herbert Read writes:

The echoes of my life which I find in my early childhood are too many to be dismissed as vain coincidences; but it is perhaps my conscious life which is the echo, the only real experiences in life being those lived with a virgin sensibility—*so that we only hear a tone once, only see a colour once, see, hear, touch, taste and smell everything once, the first time.* All life is an echo of our first sensations, and we build up our consciousness, our whole mental life, by variations and combinations of these elementary sensations. But it is more complicated than that, for the senses apprehend not only colours and tones and shapes, but also patterns and atmospheres, and our first discovery of these determines the larger patterns and subtler atmospheres of all our subsequent existence.

Once, then, we experienced wholeness, once we perceived form, movement, color, light, and expression in one completely satisfying form.

* Rudolf Koch, *The Book of Signs* (translated by Vyvyan Holland)

The infant, in his small universe of home and family, learns first to fasten his hopes on the constellations of eyes which meet his, and he guides his course by their responsive signals. In later years he focuses on the distant, unattainable light of the stars as symbols of hope, serenity, and steadfastness, and his trust in them may well prove to have been determined by the trustworthiness and constant light in the eyes which first met his in the mutuality of giving and receiving.

We have, then, the eyes, the stars and the man-made bead—the eyes without which the world is a lonely waste, the stars without which the sky becomes a black and frightening void—and the man-made bead, the shining sphere which can be worn on the person and thus kept close and safe. The heavens may cloud over, the eyes will close, but there is comfort in the durable symbol, the constancy of beads.

Chinese character for bead and for pupil of the eye

Opposite page, Choker and Earrings—gold and Pre-Columbian jade
(Mexico)

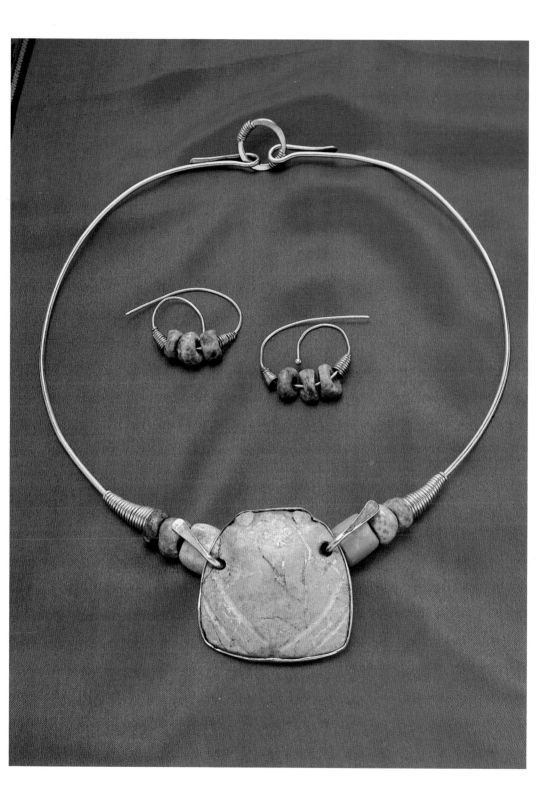

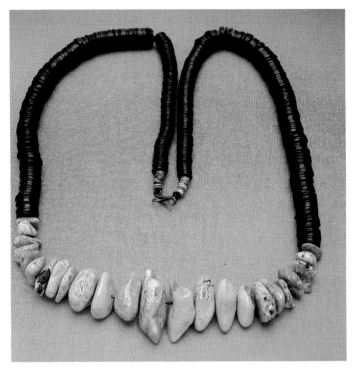

Necklace—turquoise (Arizona) and coconut shell disks (Africa)

Donkey Beads—blue glass trade beads strung with wooden dividers (Far East)

Necklace—amber (Russia)

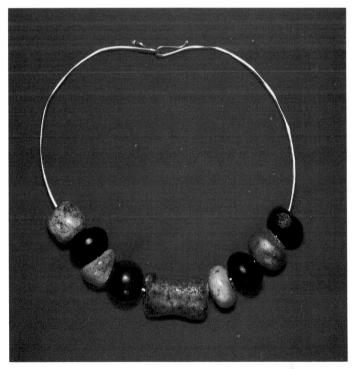

Beads—Pre-Columbian jade (Mexico)

Necklace—ancient Peruvian beads

Necklace—carnelian and silver (Indonesia)

Wooden Prayer Beads (Far East)

Blue Glass Beads and Bells (Africa)

Camel's Nose Ring (Middle East)

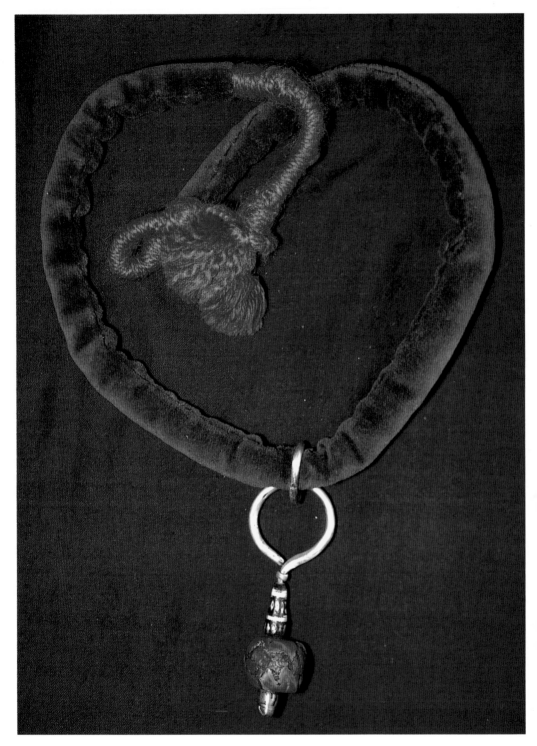

Mule-driver's Earring (Tibet)

Index

Page numbers in italics refer to illustrations; page numbers followed by *n* refer to footnotes.